WOKE
injustice

A Biblical Response to Critical Race Theory

Bryan Osborne

First printing: September 2024

New Leaf Press, P.O. Box 726, Green Forest, AR 72638

New Leaf Press is a division of the New Leaf Publishing Group, LLC.

ISBN: 978-1-68344-372-8
ISBN: 978-1-61458-891-7 (digital)

Library of Congress Control Number: 2024943903

Cover and interior design: Diana Bogardus

Printed in the United States of America

New Leaf Press
A Division of New Leaf Publishing Group
www.newleafpress.com

Please visit our website for other titles: www.newleafpress.com

For information regarding promotional opportunities, please contact the publicity department at pr@nlpg.com.

What Other People Are Saying ～

"I am astonished that you are…turning to a different gospel" (Galatians 1:6). The early church faced the same problems we do today—false teaching that morphs the true gospel into a different gospel altogether, a gospel Paul says isn't a gospel at all! Wokeism and social justice are some of today's pervasive false teachings that threaten the church. In this book, Bryan has done a skillful job exposing this compromise and returning Christians to the truth and authority of God's Word.

—Ken Ham
CEO/founder of Answers in Genesis,
Creation Museum, and Ark Encounter

Critical Race Theory and its various companions in the "woke" worldview are taking the West by storm, ushering in a new post-Christian era. Bryan has written a gospel-focused, relevant, and enlightening guidebook for the Christian who wants to maintain "transformed" rather than "conformed" thinking (Rom 12:2) in this new world. This is essential knowledge.

—Martyn Iles
Answers in Genesis Executive CEO

The underlying agenda of Critical Theory has been sealed behind the moat of obscure jargon and flown under the banner of justice. Inquiries at her towers are promptly restrained by pawns armed with cancel culture. This highly guarded social movement compels the use of "newspeak" wherein any nonconformity is an oppressor's admission. Osborne's *Woke Injustice* carefully extinguishes the heat and defangs the rhetoric of the debate by exposing the unbiblical and ultimately unjust aims of Social Justice. He proves how Scripture offers the only leveling ground, and justification by faith lived out biblically is the only path to any true justice in our lost world.

— Joe Owens
AiG Latin America Director and Speaker

CRITICAL RACE THEORY
undermines the character of individuals by perpetuating prejudice and injustice, rather than promoting true equality.

... *"For the Lord sees not as man sees: man looks on the outward appearance, but the Lord looks on the heart."*
(1 Samuel 16:7)

Character cannot thrive with injustice; nor can equality be achieved through prejudice.

Terms like woke, CRT, social justice, equity, etc. fill headlines spelling doom and gloom for those who don't embrace their supposed reality and live out these new "truths." Sadly, many Christians have bowed the knee, made apologies, and denied the truth of God's Word beginning in Genesis. *Woke Injustice* is a toolbox for Christians to equip them to discern wrong thinking, defend biblical truth, and most importantly speak the truth in love. Bryan unpacks the ideas of the cultural left with clarity and hope pointing to the all-sufficient God and His Word.

—Dr. Georgia Purdom
VP of Educational Content for Answers in Genesis, Speaker, Writer

Table of Contents

Dedication and Acknowledgments

Truly and eternally, all the glory belongs to my Creator, God, Lord and Savior, Jesus Christ. His kindness, grace, and power are profoundly displayed in the creation of this book. My primary hope is that He is exalted through this work.

Anyone who knows me knows that I call my wife my greatest earthly blessing, because she is! Marla, I love you beyond words and you are the most vivid picture of Christ to me and our children on a daily basis. I could not have a better best friend, spouse, and ministry partner. I cannot thank God enough for the blessings He continually pours into our lives through you.

Once again, my incredible children were at the forefront of my mind as I wrote this book. Ian, you are growing up to be an amazing young man and I could not be prouder that you are my son. Macie, you are remarkably beautiful in every way, and I'm ever so thankful that you will always be daddy's girl. I love you both more than you could ever imagine. It is

my greatest hope that both of you know, enjoy, serve, and glorify Jesus! That you will find your identity in the only place where it can be truly found — in Christ.

My wife and children are my greatest earthly blessings, and I cannot imagine this book existing without them. God has used them in such a wonderful way to inspire, direct, teach, mold, and motivate me in life and in the endeavor of this work. I praise You, Lord, for who You are, what You have done, are doing, and will do, and for the blessing of my family. May Jesus Christ be glorified to the uttermost!

Introduction

Why It Matters

What's the big deal about critical race theory — CRT? Why does Answers in Genesis care? Why should Christians (and non-Christians) care about an idea that for so long has seemingly only resounded in the halls of higher academia?

Well, for starters, CRT is a new face on an old idea whose purpose is societal division and destruction. CRT graduated from the college classroom long ago and has spread to every corner of our society. Unfortunately, it's featured in schools, corporations, media, government agencies, politics, and many Christian institutions. It goes by many deceptive names and is propagandized by various lofty sounding phrases. As we'll see later, its presence is not benign, nor is CRT a "helpful analytical tool" as some have called it. It is a malignant cancer, spreading animosity and injustice wherever it is found with devastating effects if left unchecked.

The reason CRT is so pernicious is that its driving ideology is utterly anti-biblical. Consequently, CRT undermines biblical authority, sufficiency of Scripture, biblical anthropology (right understanding of people), and gospel sufficiency. CRT's chief function and goal is to instigate division and to tear down and rebuild under a new authority. If that sounds like a bad thing to bring into the church, that's because it is. Yet somehow, various tenets of the CRT dogma have infiltrated the minds of many Christian leaders, churches, and Christian organizations. This is why this issue should profoundly matter to Christians and why we at Answers in Genesis, a biblical authority ministry, care so much about it. If we desire human flourishing, unity, and real reconciliation, we should care. If we desire for God to be glorified through the right understanding, submission to, and application of His Word, we should care.

On a personal note, once I understood CRT's sinister lies, I realized the immense danger it poses to how people, including Christians, view their identity. I wanted to equip myself, my family, my kids, and the body of Christ wherever I could, with the biblical reality of who we are, that we would be able to distinguish biblical truth from the incessant noise of our cultural voices. That we have the proper understanding of our identity as God's image bearers, that our problem is sin, and the gospel is the answer. This is the identity and reality of every human ever, no matter their skin shade. And it is this revelation of Scripture that the Church must cling to and engage the culture with.

What This Book Is Not

To be clear, this book is not an analysis of the racist evils of America's past. No rational, informed person would argue against the historical realities of the heinous injustices of slavery, segregation, discrimination, Jim Crow laws, etc. Unfortunately, those things really happened. They were entirely evil and anti-biblical (though some professing Christians twisted Scripture like the devil in his temptation of Jesus to justify their unbiblical beliefs).

Answers in Genesis has repeatedly addressed many of these atrocious realities in various resources. As I travel and speak, I often discuss some of these horrors as they typically stem from a secular, evolutionary ideology that equates people to worms. I mean, if people are just animals, then why not abuse, enslave, and discard them for your own benefit? Darwin clearly stated that some humans were more evolved than others.[1] And it's all about survival of the fittest, right? Make no mistake, it was Christians that led the abolition of slavery, and many other injustices, in the west and around the world. They were driven by the biblical reality that every human being is made in God's image and thus has indelible, equal, eternal value.

---

1 For example, in his book *The Descent of Man* Darwin said, "At some future period … the civilized races [light skinned] of man will almost certainly exterminate and replace the savage races [dark skinned] throughout the world." Charles Darwin, *The Descent of Man* (Chicago, IL: William Benton in Great Books of the Western World, 1952), p. 336.

It also cannot be logically or historically denied that those appalling injustices had multi-generational consequences. And of course, no sane person would argue that racism and injustice have been completely purged from America, or anywhere else in the world. This world is an unjust place because it is filled with unjust sinners like you and me. All these historic realities are no doubt extremely important but are not the focus of this book.

What This Book Is

This book is addressing the question, is CRT the answer? Is it the answer to those historic tragedies, their effects, and the racial reconciliation issues of today? Is it at the very least a "helpful, analytical tool"? Is woke justice actual justice? Spoiler alert: as we shall see, the answer to all these questions is a resounding no! But don't worry, in the mist of all the cultural distortions and lies, there is a right answer. We'll see that it comes from the place where all right answers are fundamentally found — the authoritative, transformative, sufficient Word of the living God. It is His Word that leads us to the true justice and unity found solely in the gospel of Jesus Christ.

Some may ask why this book when there already exist many good books on this issue? Indeed, there are some superb resources that thoroughly

address the issue of CRT. Incredible, in-depth books like *Fault Lines* by Voddie Bauchaum, which is a stunning dissection of the social justice movement and its impact on evangelicalism. Or *Christianity and Wokeness* by Owen Strachen, which is a powerful exposé of woke ideology. The "Just Thinking Podcast" featuring Darrell Harrison and Virgil Walker is a phenomenal long-form podcast where each episode is like listening to a carefully researched book. In episode 108 they give a remarkable analysis of CRT. I am indebted to each of these, and others, for helping me to think biblically on this subject and I highly recommend them.

But again, each of those great resources dives deep. Like my previous two books, *Quick Answers to Tough Questions* and *Quick Answers to Social Issues,* the aim of this book is to deliver concise, biblical answers. Clear answers that can be shared with your children, a family member, friend, coworker, neighbor, or a congregation. This is done by boiling CRT down to its core components, taking away its fabricated mystique and removing its undeserved intimidation, then applying the Christian worldview to provide a straightforward understanding and rebuttal of CRT. This arms Christians with the necessary, practical answers to combat the insidious "justice" of *Woke Injustice*.[2]

---

2   Broadly, to be "woke" means being awake to the (supposed) reality that society systemi-
    cally oppresses racial and sexual minorities, causing inequities and injustice as defined by
    neo-Marxism/CRT. As we'll see, "woke injustice" often calls what is evil good and good evil;
    advancing injustice in the name of justice.

Laying the Foundation: Worldviews, Neutrality, and Faith

1

To properly analyze and discuss CRT, it is crucial to lay the proper groundwork. Every ideology comes from a worldview built on a foundational authority. But to understand this and its implications to our examination of CRT we must first define what a worldview is.

In short, a worldview is how we view the world (I know, mind blowing right?). It is a collection of our most basic beliefs about reality. It's literally impossible to function without a worldview. Everyone, whether they realize it or not, admit it or not, like it or not, has a worldview. It's all the things we presume to be true as we engage, interpret, and respond to the world around us. These assumptions, and the culminating worldview, are assumed before looking at the world, and become the lens through which all of reality is understood.

To use a classic illustration, if someone has "blue tinted worldview glasses" then everything in the world will look blue to them. If they have "red tinted worldview glasses" then it all appears to be red. It's not that everything is necessarily all blue or all red. Quite the opposite could be true. Rather, that is how it appears and is interpreted by the viewer because of the tint of his lens based on the assumptions that comprise his worldview.

This is why two people can look at the exact same facts and reach such drastically different conclusions. As a ministry that deals directly with the origins debate, we see this all the time. A scientist with an evolutionary worldview will look at the fossil record and conclude billions of years of death and change, transforming primordial soup into all of life's diversity. Another scientist, with a consistent biblical worldview, will interpret the same fossil record as amazing evidence for the global Flood that occurred roughly 4,400 years ago. Same evidence. Two extremely different interpretations. Why? Different worldviews.

The exact same thing is true for all of today's social issues. Different people can look at the same issues of gender, sexuality, racism, justice, racial reconciliation, etc. and get radically different conclusions. Why? You guessed it — different worldviews.

Here's the key: What's ultimately happening is a battle over authority because every worldview is built on, and sustained by, a foundational authority. And friends, fundamentally there are only two authorities to choose from: God's or man's. On any and every issue, either God's Word is your authority or man's word is. Do you put your faith in the contradictory ideas of finite, sinful, broken people? Or do you trust the revelation of the living God who is eternal, infinite, all-knowing, all-powerful, unchanging, perfect, always loving, always truthful, always good, and always just? It is solely from one of these two foundations that every individual must construct their thinking and worldview.

Also understand, when someone rejects God's Word, they're left with man's arbitrary ideas from which they must choose to create their own worldview. Thus, the individual becomes the ultimate authority defining truth for himself, becoming his own god. Trust God or *"you will be like god,"* a lie as old as Genesis 3 (Genesis 3:5).

That being said, all worldviews are not created equal. Connecting back to our earlier illustration, this is not a battle between equally valid but differently "tinted" worldviews. Every worldview built on man's word is utterly corrupted by sin, which blurs and skews the adherent's view of reality. A biblical worldview built from God's Word is much more than "tinted glasses"; it is corrective lenses.

Ever since I can remember I've been awfully near-sighted but wasn't diagnosed and prescribed glasses until I was around 10. Before then, the whole world beyond seven feet away was a literal blur. I just assumed that was normal and that's how it looked to everyone else. I would frequently misinterpret things or miss them altogether because my vision was so poor. Then I got glasses, and everything changed. For the first time I saw the world around me as it really was! I could see individual leaves in trees, the teacher's writing on the board, people's facial expressions that communicate so much but that I had largely remained oblivious to. My broken vision distorted my view of the world, and I needed corrective lenses.

That is what God's Word does for us. Each person is born with a spiritual sight problem called sin. It is the truth of Scripture and a biblical worldview, empowered by the Holy Spirit, which act as corrective lenses, bringing the world into clarity, repairing our sin-cursed vision to rightly see and respond to reality.

But if someone rejects God's Word, starting with wrong assumptions rooted in the warped vision of man's ideas, they will likely get the wrong conclusions. This is why so many seemingly intelligent people can be so wrong about issues ranging from sexuality, racism, justice, or the age of the earth. Wrong foundation, wrong worldview, wrong interpretations, wrong conclusions.

And don't fall for today's ever so popular lie that you should be neutral. It cannot be overstated — neutrality does not exist. Every worldview not resting on the rock of God's eternally perfect Word is resting on the shifting sand of man's fallible, finite ideas. Everyone makes a choice, whether they realize it or not, to submit and live according to one of these foundational authorities. Scripture says, *"For the mind that is set on the flesh is hostile to God"* (Romans 8:7) and *"friendship with the world is enmity [hostility] with God?"* (James 4:4). In Matthew 12:30 Jesus declared, *"Whoever is not with me is against me, and whoever does not gather with me scatters."* Scripture is crystal clear — no one can be neutral. Neutrality is biblically impossible. So, to claim someone can be neutral, is to say the Bible is wrong, which is to be anti-biblical and therefore not neutral.

Here are a couple of things to remember when someone asks you to be neutral: **1. they're not** and **2. you can't be.** Nor should you pretend to be. It must be recognized that every contested issue boils down to a battle of authority between the Word of God and the word of man. And if a Christian, in the name of "neutrality," agrees the Bible isn't needed for truth on any issue, he's just conceded that man's word is supreme. By doing that, he's lost the argument at the foundational level before it ever got started. All of today's societal disputes, including CRT and "social justice," are actually "authority battles," and you cannot defend biblical authority by abandoning biblical authority! *Rather, Christians are to unashamedly hold fast to God's Word* (2 Timothy 2:24–25), *taking every thought captive to obedience to Christ* (2 Corinthians 10:5), *always being prepared to give a defense with gentleness and respect* (1 Peter 3:15), *using Scripture to exhort and rebuke those who contradict, in the hope that people will get saved* (Titus 1:9)!

Now the secularists will argue, "You've got faith, but we've got facts." But they're wrong on two counts. First, we've all got the same facts — facts that must be interpreted with a worldview. Second, the unbeliever has faith too. Do not miss this — everyone has faith! The question is where do you put it? Again, there are only two options. Either you put your faith in God's Word or, if you reject that, by default you're putting your faith in man's word.

Faith placed in man's arbitrary, finite word, which assumes no God (or no consistently revealed God), leads to many absurd beliefs. For example, you essentially must believe everything came from nothing, order naturally came from chaos, information came from inanimate matter, and life came from non-life — all of which violates multiple, well-established laws of science. Also consider, if there is no God, how does one explain the existence of non-tangible realities like logic, knowledge, truth, justice, absolute morality, or natural laws? If evolution is true and everything changes over time, why don't the laws of nature and logic randomly change? If there is no God and no moral absolutes, what is justice and why should anyone care about it?

Man's ideas are limited, broken, contradictory, and incapable of self-consistently explaining all the facets of reality both material and immaterial. As a result, faith placed in man's ideas is an irrational blind faith. Whereas the biblical faith is a rational, cogent faith.

Only the biblical worldview can self-consistently explain all of reality. It can explain the beauty in creation and the intricacies of design as the work of our all-powerful, wise Creator (Genesis 1–2). The brokenness and pain of this world is explained by man's fall into sin and the rightful resulting consequences warned of by the just Judge (Genesis 3). Scripture explains why we long for something beyond this world (Ecclesiastes 3:11), and what God has done to make all things new (Revelation 21:5).

The Bible alone provides a coherent reason for the existence of universal, unchanging, immaterial things, like the laws of logic, laws of nature, and absolute morality. Things that cannot be seen, tasted, or touched but are unequivocally real and necessary to function in this world. These things come from, and are sustained by, our eternal, unchanging, omnipresent God who is Spirit and is not limited by His creations of time, space, and matter. Why do humans intuitively know and use these immaterial realities? Why do humans innately desire justice? Because we are made in the Creator's image. The One who made and upholds all of reality for our good and His glory. The bottom line is, although everyone has faith, only the Christian faith self-consistently makes sense of everything.

Now, with the proper foundation laid, we're ready to dive into CRT. As we do, the two primary questions are these:

1. Does CRT come from the foundation of **God's Word** or man's?

2. Will Christians trust that God and His Word are **sufficient** for all of life, godliness, and equipping believers for every good work (2 Peter 1:3; 2 Timothy 3:16–17)?

2

CRT: Its Definition and Origin

What Is It?

Critical Race Theory, commonly called CRT for short, is popping up everywhere in our culture; but what is it? Just a quick Google search for CRT's definition leads to various explanations, often long and confusing. So here's a concise, summative definition that will be fleshed out throughout the following chapters:

> CRT is a **worldview** that assumes a society is made up of oppressors and the oppressed, primarily according to "race." It assumes the oppressors have structured society to their benefit, to suppress the oppressed, and thus the society is **systemically oppressive** (racist).

CRT is an all-encompassing worldview, as its creators and proponents clearly intend and often state. The UCLA Luskin School of Public Affairs, a primary definer of CRT today, says this when defining CRT:

> CRT recognizes [assumes] that racism is engrained in the fabric and system of the American society…. This is the analytical lens [worldview] that CRT uses in examining existing power structures.[1]

Please note their admission that CRT **takes for granted** that "racism is engrained in … American society." It is the assumption of systemic oppression and racism that serves as the "analytical lens" for CRT. In other words, CRT is not some kind of secondary, analytical tool that can be used by your worldview — CRT is a worldview. It is not meant to be proven; it is presumed. If blue tinted glasses represented the CRT worldview, anyone who donned those glasses would see all of reality with a blueish tint. You wouldn't put those glasses on to determine if

---

1   "What Is Critical Race Theory?," UCLA School of Public Affairs, Critical Race Studies, http://spacrs.wordpress.com/what-is-critical-race-theory.

everything is blue. On the contrary, you put those glasses on and then, you see everything as blue. Likewise, CRT is intended to be the lens through which all of society is seen. It doesn't simply analyze reality, it defines it.

Where Did It Come From?

CRT is an evolved form of Marxism. Marxism came from the ideas and writings of a German-born philosopher named Karl Marx who lived in the mid 1800s. Marx's theories also served as a basis for communism which is why he has been called "The Father of Communism." Long story short, Marx viewed history and defined society as a battle between social classes. A battle between those with power, the oppressors, and those who were being exploited, the oppressed. This is called Marx's "Conflict Theory." This thinking is prominently displayed in Marx's Communist Manifesto, which he co-authored with Friedrich Engels:

> The history of all hitherto existing society is the history of class struggles. Freeman and slave … lord and serf, guild-master and journeyman, in a word, oppressor and oppressed.[2]

In Marx's day, he deemed the oppressors to be the wealthy class (the bourgeoisie) and the oppressed were the poor working class (the proletariat). Since Marx believed capitalism to be intrinsically unstable, he expected that the oppressed would eventually recognize their exploitation and work together to overthrow their oppressors. He believed a revolution, not reform, was necessary. The goal was not to modify an existing societal structure, rather to tear that structure down in order to "build back better," if you will. Marx predicted that a societal utopia, with no ruling class, would eventually bloom after the revolution of the oppressed. Everyone would then work selflessly in harmony, creating a society where individuals could most fully express their authentic humanity.

But after the workers' revolutions failed to destroy capitalism by the early 1900s, a new generation of Marxists began asking questions. Why didn't

---

2   Karl Marx and Friedrich Engels, *The Communist Manifesto,* Chapter I, Bourgeois and Proletarians, https://www.marxists.org/archive/marx/works/1848/communist-manifesto/ch01.htm.

the oppressed revolt the way Marx anticipated and bring about the grand revolution? What went wrong? What renovations needed to be made to Marxism to make it "work"?

Enter an Italian Marxist named Antonio Gramsci. He concluded that Marx's revolution never properly occurred because of a problem he called "hegemony." In a nutshell, hegemony is the idea that society's ruling group, the oppressors, establish the "rules of the game." They structure society to always benefit them and to oppress all others. So, the oppression is not merely between different groups, it's actually ingrained into the institutions of society and society itself. Since the oppressed know nothing different than the oppressive system they live in, they assume that system is normative. Thus, oppression is normalized and the reason the oppressed never properly revolted is because they were not awake to their oppression. For the revolution to be successful, the oppressed must first awaken to their oppression and the systemic oppression entrenched in their society.

If the idea of hegemony seems a bit nebulous, maybe this will help. My son Ian, who is 10 at the time of this writing, has always loved to make up his own games. There are rules, progressions, props, rewards, the works. Of course, he gets the rest of the family to play his games with him and we have a good time. But here's the rub. Guess who always wins Ian's games? Ian! It never fails. Somehow, he always finds a way to structure,

utilize, or change, the rules of his game so that he is always the victor. This is hegemony.

Continuing the analogy, if Ian teaches his younger sister Macie his game, with his rules, and that's all she knows, she'll assume it's all normal. Though she may lose every time she'll assume that's just the way it is, whether she likes it or not, so why fight against it. Ian's "systemic oppression" has been normalized. This is hegemony, and, might I add, the cutest possible example of it. This is what Gramsci added to the Marxist equation.

Then along comes the Frankfurt School, initiated primarily by a famous group of Marxists out of Frankfurt, Germany. Essentially, they fine-tuned Marxist ideas, modifying and adding in elements like hegemony. They rejected some of Marx's main economic assumptions but kept his basic conflict theory, which they expanded and applied to all of society. The culmination of their work is called Critical Theory. It basically asserts:

≫ All of society boils down to oppressor versus oppressed.

≫ The oppressors have all societal power and dominate other groups.

≫ Society is systemically oppressive and broken.

≫ The goal is to address oppressive societal structures, returning power to the oppressed in the quest for equity and "social justice."

CRT: Its Definition and Origin

As time went on, many of their members infiltrated college classrooms as professors, working as evangelists for their version of Neo (new)-Marxism.[3]

Note that their use of the words "Critical Theory" have specific meanings and application. "Critical" is not meant in the analytical sense, like to think critically and evaluate. Their intended meaning is to be critical of, to repudiate, to criticize with the purpose of exposing societal problems to awaken the oppressed, hoping to cause a revolution to accomplish their desired change. "Theory" is not meant in the sense of a hypothetical idea or guess that needs to be verified. In their use, "Theory" is a capitalized proper noun. In this context, it is a set of **assumed** ideas that **guide** thought and practice. In other words, it is a worldview, not a "helpful analytical tool."

Finally, critical theorists toss in the middle of the words "Critical Theory" whatever they believe to be a primary systemic cultural problem. So, you get intimidating titles such as:

≫ Critical Legal Theory   ≫ Critical Queer Theory

≫ Critical Class Theory   ≫ Critical Race Theory

≫ Critical Gender Theory   ≫ And so on.

Of course, with America's history of racially based slavery, segregation, and discrimination, racism is seen as its core systemic problem. And presto, you've got Critical Race Theory.

Although Marx rightly identified some real problems, he hypothesized wrong causes and painfully wrong solutions because of his atheistic worldview. In the end, he utterly rejected Christianity, God, and the Bible and instead developed his thinking on the foundation of man's ideas, primarily his own. The Bible says that the fear of the Lord is the beginning of knowledge (Proverbs 1:7) and that all the treasures of wisdom and

3   Martin Jay, *The Dialectical Imagination: A History of the Frankfurt School and the Institute of Social Research 1923-1950* (London: Heinemann, 1973), p. 284. A PDF of the book is available at https://newsfollowup.com/docs/cm9-11/docs/gen/dialetical-immagination-martin-jay.pdf.

knowledge are found in Christ (Colossians 2:3). In their arrogance, Marx and his disciples have rejected the only source of truth and wisdom and have concocted a destructive worldview mired in foolishness.

Marxism, old and new, gets the fundamentals of humanity catastrophically wrong. It sees things like traditional biblical morality, the family unit, and Christianity as major parts of systemic oppression. It says humans are a product of nature, their identity is either oppressor or oppressed, their problem is oppression, and the solution is revolution. The Bible says humans are the crowning jewel of God's creation, their identities are as individuals made in the Creator's image, their problem is sin, and their solution is Christ. In the end, these two worldviews are resting on two different foundations and are diametrically opposed to each other.

What is CRT? A new variation of atheistic, anti-Christian Marxism. Where does Marxism come from? Ultimately, it's an offshoot of the religion of humanism, an ideology that places its focus on, and supreme faith in, humanity. Simply put, the Neo-Marxist creed of CRT comes from man's word, not God's. Matthew 7:17–18 reminds us,

> So, every healthy tree bears good fruit, but the diseased tree
> bears bad fruit. A healthy tree cannot bear bad fruit, nor
> can a diseased tree bear good fruit.

Friends, anything built on the foundation of man's word is a branch from a "diseased tree." Ideas have consequences and bad ideas have victims. Christians would be wise to heed the warning of Colossians 2:8:

> See to it that no one takes you captive by philosophy
> and empty deceit, according to human tradition,
> according to the elemental spirits of the world,
> and not according to Christ.

3

8 Core Principles of CRT

With CRT's definition and origin in place, I want to provide what I have estimated to be the 8 core principles of CRT. This is a big picture summary of CRT's basic tenets and the best way I have found to concisely communicate the realities of CRT ideology. Of course, this list could be expanded, and each principle further expounded, but this is meant to get to the nitty-gritty of this Neo-Marxist creed. These principles will be elaborated on later. After these dogmas have been articulated, we will see throughout the rest of the book how they are pervasively showing up in the culture and the church.

1. **People are identified by groups according to race, ethnicity, religion, sexuality, etc., as either an oppressor or the oppressed.**

In CRT, all people do not have indelible, equivalent value bestowed on them by God. Nor are people identified as individuals who are responsible and accountable, at least to some degree, defined by their own choices, actions, words, and character. A mix of positive and negative characteristics with the possibility of improvement or decline. Nope, none of that. Simply, if you look like this, have those particular traits, or have these feelings, you are a repugnant oppressor, or an innocent oppressed one. You are categorically assigned to one of those two groups whether you know it or not, whether you like it or not. Think about how contradictory this is to biblical anthropology on multiple levels. The Bible says in Genesis 1:27,

> *So God created man in his own image, in the image of God*
> *he created him; male and female he created them.*

The Bible unequivocally declares that every individual has equal, inherent value because each person bears the image of the living God.

The Bible also repeatedly states that each individual is accountable before God for their own sin. In Romans 14:11–12 we read,

> For it is written, "As I live, says the Lord, every knee shall bow to me, and every tongue shall confess to God." So then **each** of us will give and account of **himself** to God [emphasis bold italics mine].

In regard to being defined by character, actions, and words, Proverbs is filled to the brim with comparisons between the "wise man" and the "fool."

> The way of a fool is right in his own eyes, but a wise man listens to advice (Proverbs 12:15).

> The simple believes everything, but the prudent gives thought to his steps. One who is wise is cautious and turns away from evil, but a fool is reckless and careless (Proverbs 14:15–16).

> A fool gives full vent to his spirit [anger], but a wise man quietly holds it back (Proverbs 29:11).

And since all humans descend from Adam, inheriting a sin nature, every person is fundamentally defined as a sinner and part of the problem.

> For all have sinned and fall short of the glory of God (Romans 3:23).

It's because of this biblical reality that each person equally needs saving through the Last Adam Jesus Christ.

> For as by a man came death, by a man has come also the resurrection of the dead. For as in Adam all die, so also in Christ shall all be made alive (1 Corinthians 15:21–22).

The Bible says humanity is united in its origin, value, sin problem, and need for a Savior. CRT asserts that we are categorically and irreparably divided into oppressed and oppressors. These two views of identity, societal problems, and the suggested corresponding solutions could not be more different. Either you put your faith in God's Word or man's.

2. **Intersectionality is the tool used by the Critical Theorist to determine someone's group and level of oppression.**

In short, intersectionality is the idea that there are intersecting and compounding layers of cultural oppression due to multiple factors like race, gender, sexuality, etc. The more victim categories someone falls into, the heavier their oppression, and thus the greater societal empowerment they deserve. For example, a woman's voice should be more culturally authoritative than a man's because she has experienced oppression as a woman that the man cannot. If that woman is also African American, she's to be even more empowered because she has also experienced oppression as an ethnic minority. If she's also lesbian, she has even more authority and is deserving of more reparations because of her additional experienced oppression as a sexual minority. If she's also transgender... well you get the idea.

But how do you know if you're oppressed and by "how much"? What are the categories of oppression that intersect and compound? In general, Critical Theorists classify it this way:

The Oppressors	The Oppressed
White, male, heterosexual, cisgender (identify by birth gender), able-bodied, colonialists, Christian	Non-white, female, homosexual, transgender, disabled, indigenous, non-Christian

Note that with CRT, race is the primary oppressive issue but not the only one the Neo-Marxists seek to exploit. Critical Theorists cast a wide net seeking to comprehensively deconstruct a society in the name of revolution.

3. **Oppression is the only real sin, only the oppressors are guilty, and it is systemically present.**

There are so many things wrong with this core CRT dogma. According to CRT, the only real iniquity in a society is oppression. But one must ask, with no God and absolute standard for morality, how can it authoritatively be stated that oppression is wrong. We don't get mad at lions for "oppressing" the antelope. You may have a preference against your arbitrary definition of oppression, but how dare you intolerantly demand that everyone abandon their beliefs for yours! That's bigoted, hateful, narrow-minded, and offensive — you're canceled.

Christians, however, have a consistent reason as to why genuine oppression is wrong. Every human is equally made in the Creator's image (Genesis 1:27) and God commands His image bearers to show no partiality.

> *But if you show partiality, you are committing sin and are*
> *convicted by the law as transgressors (James 2:9).*

The "Golden Rule" in Matthew 7:12 instructs us to treat others the way we want to be treated. The biblical worldview alone consistently provides the basis for seeking to correct unbiblical partiality and oppression wherever it may be found. But the Bible is equally clear

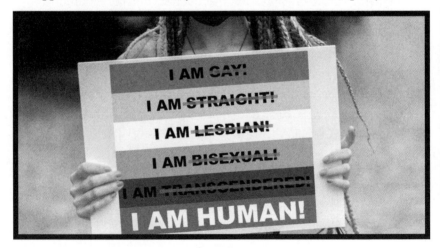

that partiality is not the only sin, nor are those guilty of it the only sinners. Again, all have sinned and fall short of God's glory (Romans 3:23). This is another way CRT dramatically misses the mark and is in severe conflict with Christianity.

CRT profoundly rejects the biblical reality that sin is the ultimate problem for society and every individual. Instead, it deems certain identity groups, the oppressors, as the problem leaving the oppressed as innocent by CRT definition. Morality is not defined by the Creator, revealing a conflict between a good God and rebellious people. It is arbitrarily defined in terms of "good" and "bad" identity groups. In CRT, if you have the designated traits of the "oppressor group," you are bad by definition, prejudged as guilty. It doesn't care about your love for others, your family's origin, character, words, or actions. This is quite the opposite of God's just judgment which defines and condemns oppression and injustice in relation to sinful actions, words, and attitudes.

On the flip side, the oppressed are prejudged as innocent no matter what they say or do. And anything they do to fight against their oppressors and oppression is justified. This is why, for example, so many students and faculty from CRT-saturated universities vehemently praised and supported Hamas after its October 7, 2023, massacre.[1] It didn't matter that Hamas murdered over 1,200 innocent Jews, the deadliest attack against the Jewish people since the Holocaust. It didn't matter that Hamas had brutally butchered babies, raped women, burned families alive, or took hundreds hostage. Why didn't it matter? Because the Jews were viewed as the "oppressive occupiers,"[2] while Hamas represented the "oppressed" Palestinians. Thus, Hamas was "justified" in all that it did.

---

1   Ingrid Jacques, "Harvard for Hamas? Something is very twisted on America's university campuses," USA Today, October 12, 2023, https://www.usatoday.com/story/opinion/columnist/2023/10/12/hamas-attack-harvard-students-blame-israel/71152750007/.

2   Incredibly ironic. The Jews just lived through the Holocaust in recent history. Pretty sure that would qualify them as an historically oppressed ethnic minority. If not, what does?

CRT also defines all of societies oppression as systemic. It's everywhere all the time, baked into the cake if you will. In any given situation the question is not did oppression occur, but how did it occur?

4. **Any disparity in outcome between oppressor and oppressed groups is the result of oppression/discrimination/racism. Period.**

For the oppressor or oppressed, personal choices, efforts, sacrifices, work ethic, habits, abilities, character, upbringing, cultural context, intellect, planning, preparation etc. do not matter. Your history doesn't matter. If you're an "oppressor" and your family has always been destitute, but you somehow achieve success beyond some of the "oppressed," that's oppression. If someone from the oppressed class succeeds beyond the oppressors, that's despite their oppression and is just reparation. CRT declares that any disparity in outcome is "oppressive discrimination." Everyone must receive the same outcome; the distribution of resources and power must be equal without fail. If this sounds "socialistic," that's because it is.

CRT argues that the only reason any of the "oppressors" are more successful is because the rules of society have been rigged to always benefit them. Correspondingly, the only real reason the "oppressed" are unsuccessful by comparison is the result of systemic oppression that stacks the deck against them. Demanding equivalent outcomes is a primary way the critical theorists seek to rectify "systemic discrimination."

Of course, the Bible is replete with instructions to care for those in genuine need.

> *For there will never cease to be poor in the land. Therefore*
> *I command you, "You shall open wide your hand to*
> *your brother, to the needy and to the poor, in your land"*
> *(Deuteronomy 15:11).*

> *Give justice to the weak and the fatherless; maintain the*
> *right of the afflicted and the destitute (Psalm 82:3).*

*Religion that is pure and undefiled before God the Father is
this: to visit orphans and widows in their affliction, and to
keep oneself unstained from the world (James 1:27).*

The Bible also says that if someone is able to work but chooses not to,
they don't eat.

*For even when we were with you, we would give you this
command: If anyone is not willing to work, let him not eat
(2 Thessalonians 3:10).*

And it's quite possible that many of those demanding equal outcomes
may be motivated by a desire for someone else's stuff. That's the sin
of coveting.

*You shall not covet your neighbor's house; you shall not
covet your neighbor's wife, or his male servant, or his
female servant, or his ox, or his donkey, or anything that is
your neighbor's (Exodus 20:17).*

5. **The oppressed have an understanding of reality through their
oppression that the oppressors can't have. Therefore, oppressed
voices are to be culturally authoritative.**

CRT teaches that knowledge is socially constructed and there is no
objective truth. (So is that objectively true?) Once again, no objective
truth means no objective morality; that means justice cannot even be
defined, much less defended. But back to the CRT story. The decisive
determinant for truth within the CRT worldview is experience.
The oppressed gain a deeper understanding of reality through their
experience of oppression that the oppressors simply can't have. Many
have rightly compared this to a form of Gnosticism, a special enlightened knowledge known only to a select few. Thus, the oppressed, with
their elevated knowledge and clearer perception of reality, should be
listened to and followed as the ultimate cultural authority for truth.

Here's the major problem. Experience does indeed teach, but it
does not determine truth, nor does it necessarily purify the one

who endured it. For absolute truth, from an unchanging, perfectly good source, we go to God's Word. God is truth and His Word is the authority, not man's experience.

> *Forever, O Lord, your word is firmly fixed in the heavens (Psalm 119:89).*

> *The sum [entirety] of your word is truth, and every one of your righteous rules endures forever (Psalm 119:160).*

> *Jesus said to him, "I am the way, and the truth, and the life. No one comes to the Father except through me" (John 14:6).*

6. **Any who disagree with CRT are only trying to maintain oppressive power, are deceived, or are blind to their own oppression.**

Remember, as a worldview CRT is presumed not proven. Everything is to be understood through this Neo-Marxist tinted lens. According to CRT, oppressors must agree that they are oppressors or if they disagree that displays their oppression. Likewise, the oppressed will always agree that they are oppressed. If they do not, their oppression has been "normalized" and they've not yet awakened to the reality of

Gaza encampment at Columbia University protesting the "oppression" by Israel.

their subjugation. Either way, oppression is always demonstrated, and CRT is always "right."

This is a logical fallacy called assuming the conclusion: where an argument's premises simply assume the truth of the conclusion rather than supporting it.[3] The assumption is smuggled into the argument rather than proven by it. Here's a silly example, "It's an amazing fact that all elephants are green. If you don't believe elephants are green, you don't know elephants." This argument merely assumes elephants are green; it doesn't prove it. Thus, it is arbitrary and not a sound argument. The same is true for this CRT reasoning.

This argument is also evidence of the core CRT principle mentioned earlier that no matter what, the oppressors are guilty and the oppressed innocent.

7. **Power, privilege, authority, and resources must be redistributed to the oppressed.**

By CRT logic, the oppressors have illegitimately amassed wealth, power, and privilege by creating a society whose rules, structures, and institutions always benefit them. The idea of hegemony was discussed earlier. By doing this the oppressors have suppressed the oppressed, preventing them from acquiring what should have been rightfully theirs. In this sense, the oppressors have stolen from the oppressed. It is therefore morally right to transfer power, privilege, authority, and resources from the oppressors to the oppressed by whatever means deemed necessary. The goals are compensation for past systemic injustices and "leveling the playing field" of society. To accomplish this, the oppressors must be discriminated against by necessity, but that's just and a fair price to pay for appropriate reparations.

---

3   Some may say that CRT's circularity is okay because all worldviews, including Christianity, require presuppositions. But only the Christian worldview, with its foundational assumptions, provides a consistent basis for presuppositions like logic and morality. All other worldviews, including atheism/Marxism, do not. For more on this, check out this article https://answersin-genesis.org/apologetics/circular-reasoning/.

If you think this sounds like a form of socialism, you're not wrong. CRT's so-called justifications for this reallocation of resources are purely capricious presumptions that assume conclusions. In reality, they're advocating for discrimination and the forceful removal of resources from the unfavored group. That's the sin of partiality (Deuteronomy 1:17) and the sin of theft.

You shall not steal (Exodus 20:15).

8. **The solution is the deconstruction of a systemically oppressive society and a rebuilding of the society that leads to equity (not equality).**

Every good Marxist ideology requires a revolution to deconstruct and to rebuild a society, so it is with CRT. Remember, the nature of any Critical Theory is to be critical of perceived oppression. This critique is meant to draw awareness to an unjust oppression that must be remedied. And according to CRT the oppression is systemic, institutionalized, engrained in the very fiber of society. Also, the oppressors won't likely willingly give up their power, benefits, and created advantageous system. Because the oppression is so saturated into the culture, and the oppressors are so empowered by it, progressive societal reform is not a feasible option. Society is too far gone.

A London demonstration protesting government policies on cost of living and inequality.

If one really wants to redistribute power and resources to oppressed societies, the only valid option is to tear down the whole oppressive system and rebuild. As a result, CRT doesn't want to modify existing power structures; it demands deconstruction so society can be built back better. Old oppressive social structures must be abolished and replaced. There is no in-between, and there is no neutral. Either you are with the revolutionaries or against them. If you are against them, you would be wise to prepare for battle.

The end game for the revolution is to bring about equity. The CRT meaning assigned to equity is equal outcomes. Everyone gets the same stuff and same results in everything, no matter what. Recall that CRT decries any disparity in outcomes as oppressive. By equity, the critical race theorist does not mean equality. Equality assumes each person is equally valuable and worthy of equal opportunities. CRT requires equal outcomes. There's a big difference between the two.[4]

Once again, the CRT worldview unabashedly assumes these principles are true and they become the "analytical lens" used to examine, dissect, and exploit a culture. With just a glance, it should become immediately evident that CRT is not even close to biblical. In fact, as we'll see in detail later, these ideas and their necessary consequences are profoundly anti-biblical.

---

4   This distinction is so important a whole chapter is dedicated to "equity" later in the book.

CRT in America

Now let's take a look at what CRT looks like when applied to the United States. Remember, to the critical theorists, America's appalling history of race-based slavery and discrimination makes racism America's primary systemic problem. That's why Critical Race Theory is the Neo-Marxist weapon of choice against the United States. Here's a candid, concise overview of CRT's interpretation of America.

≫ **All "whites" are the oppressors.**
Individual circumstances, choices, character, efforts, or history does not matter. If you have the physical trait of "white" skin, you belong to the awful oppressor group.

≫ **"Blacks" primarily, also other minorities, are the oppressed.**
Once again, individual circumstances, choices, character, efforts, or history does not matter. If you have the physical trait of "black" skin, you belong to the innocent, victimized, oppressed group.

≫ **"Whites" have engineered society so that they are always the winners.**
This is the idea of hegemony applied to America. "Whites" built this country, with its structures and institutions, in such a way as to always benefit them. This has the added effect of continuously suppressing "blacks" as the oppressed.

≫ **Racism is systemically present in America and "whites" alone bear the guilt as oppressors.**
Because "whites" built the American society, infused with inherent bias, racism is occurring everywhere and all the time in the United States. Since only the oppressors are culpable, "whites" are guilty and "blacks" are innocent by CRT definition.

≫ **Any disparity in outcome between whites and blacks is the result of racism. Period.**

CRT demands that outcomes must be the same or it is evidence of systemic racism at work. No exceptions. Choices, efforts, habits, abilities, character, upbringing, and so on, do not play into the equation. All that matters is the "color" of your skin and the "reality" of systemic racism.

≫ **Blacks, as oppressed, have a knowledge of reality that "whites," as oppressors, cannot tap into. Therefore, black voices are to be socially authoritative.**

CRT declares that experience determines what is true in a culture. "Blacks" have acquired a deeper, "secret knowledge" about society through their experience of oppression and should be listened to as the final authority. The "white" oppressors should quietly listen, learn, and follow.

≫ **White people who disagree with CRT are being oppressively racist. Blacks who disagree with CRT are blind to their oppression and a hindrance at best.**

CRT proclaims that no matter what anyone says, "whites" are always guilty racists, and "blacks" are always innocent victims. And according

Marchers on Market Street in Union Square, San Francisco, during a rally against police violence.

to CRT logic, if you argue against systemic racism in any way, that only proves systemic racism. Isn't it amazing how all elephants are green?[1]

≫ **Power, privilege, opportunities, and resources must be reallocated: taken from whites and given to blacks and other minorities.**
"Whites," as the oppressors, have illegitimately amassed power and resources through a systemically racist and corrupt system that perpetually advantages them. Basically, directly or indirectly, "whites" have stolen from "blacks" and need to return what they've pilfered.

≫ **America is irredeemably, systemically racist. To achieve real equity, its structures, institutions — the entire society — must be deconstructed and then rebuilt in the image of CRT ideology.**
CRT asserts that America and its institutions are a lost cause, utterly beyond reform. That's why, for example, CRT advocates have not called to "reform" the police — they wanted to defund, abolish, and replace the police. This institution, like the whole society, is permeated with systemic racism and is incapable of "justice" as outlined by CRT. For the "justice" of equity to prevail, the whole thing must be torn down in order to be built back Marxist.

A Tremendously Significant Caveat

You might have noticed that the words "whites," "blacks," and even "color" have been in quotation marks all the way through this chapter. There's an important reason for that. You see, in truth there are no "black" people or "white" people; there are not different "races" of people with different "colors" of skin.

We know biblically and scientifically, there is just one race, the human race. God made Adam and Eve in His image on day six of creation week and every single human in history descends from those first two people. Thus, all humans equally bear God's image, are related to each other by blood, and are inherently equal with indelible worth. We read in Acts 17:26,

---

1   Not only is this fallaciously circular, but it is also the logical fallacy known as *Ad Hominem*. This is when an argument or reaction targets a person rather than the argument they're making. When critical race theory advocates call whites racists or blacks "Uncle Toms" for disagreeing, they're using the very discrimination they decry.

*And He has made from one blood every nation of men
to dwell on all the face of the earth, and has determined
their preappointed times and the boundaries of their
dwellings (NKJV).*

Genesis 3:20 clearly states that Eve is "the mother of all the living." In Luke 3:23–38, when Jesus' human lineage is traced backward in time, it goes all the way back to guess who — Adam, the first man. Folks, there is just one human race.

Good science confirms this reality in amazing ways. Increased research in the field of genetics has revealed that the genetic difference between any two people on earth is just 0.4% of their DNA.[2] Put another way, every person on this planet, no matter where they live, is 99.6% genetically identical! Also, mitochondrial DNA with its accumulated mutations can be traced backward through the female lineage to a common female ancestor for all females today. If you assume a standard mutation rate and that humans are only related to humans, this "Mitochondrial Eve" lived approximately 6,000 years ago![3] A similar thing can be done with the Y chromosome in males.[4] Research findings like these have even caused secular scientists to say,

> But the more closely that researchers examine the human genome — the complement of genetic material encased in the heart of almost every cell of the body — the more most of them are convinced that the standard labels used to distinguish people by "**race**" have little or no biological meaning[5] (emphasis mine).

2   National Human Genome Research Institute, Fact Sheet: "Human Genomic Variation," Last Updated: February 1, 2023, https://www.genome.gov/about-genomics/educational-resources/fact-sheets/human-genomic-variation.

3   N.T. Jeanson, 2016. "On the Origin of Human Mitochondrial DNA Differences, New Generation Time Data Both Suggest a Unified Young-Earth Creation Model and Challenge the Evolutionary Out-of-Africa Model." Answers Research Journal 9:123–130.

4   N.T. Jeanson and A.D. Holland, 2019. "Evidence for a Human Y Chromosome Molecular Clock: Pedigree-Based Mutation Rates Suggest a 4,500-Year History for Human Paternal Inheritance," Answers Research Journal 12:393–404.N.T. Jeanson, 2019. "Testing the Predictions of the Young-Earth Y Chromosome Molecular Clock: Population Growth Curves Confirm the Recent Origin of Human Y Chromosome Differences," Answers Research Journal 12:405–423.

5   Natalie Angier, "Do Races Differ? Not Really, DNA Shows," *New York Times*, Aug. 22, 2000, http://partners.nytimes.com/library/national/science/082200sci-genetics-race.html.

This one biblical, historical, and scientific truth exposes the innate idiocy of racism and, consequently, CRT. To be racist, you would have to hate your own race because there is only one. Also, for one race to oppress another race there must be different races, which don't exist. Of course, there are different ethnicities. And since Genesis 3, people of all ethnicities have found any number of sinful, often superficial, reasons to hate and harm their fellow image bearers. Just bringing home the fact that what has historically been called racism is discriminatory, ethnic hatred, because of the truth of a single human race.

People will ask, "But if there's just one race then why are people different colors?" The answer: They're not. All people are basically the same color: brown. They're just different shades of brown from dark to light. In simplified terms, this shading is mostly based on a brown pigment in human skin called melanin. If you have more melanin, you're a darker shade of brown. If you have less melanin, you're a lighter shade of brown. We're all the same color, just various shades. Our awesome God placed in Adam and Eve all the genetic information necessary to produce all the beautiful variations we see in humanity.

Some may further ask, "But why then do distinct attributes like different shades exist in different people groups?" The answer to that is the historical event of the Tower of Babel. That event separated people into isolated people groups, separated by language and geographical barriers, which

created isolated genetic pools. Within these isolated genetic pools, certain traits became dominant over time and were consistently passed down. This is genetics 101.[6]

So, I say again, there are not different "races," there are no "black" or "white" people, and there are not different "colors" of skin. There is one, gloriously diverse, human race, with each of its members bearing the Creator's image and possessing equal, eternal value. Each person also shares the common oppressive heritage of sin passed down from Adam and desperately needs to be rescued by Jesus, the Last Adam. Finally, the caveat: I'll be using the terms "blacks" and "whites" from this point forward, without quotation marks. I do not like these terms as they are biblically and scientifically inaccurate, and often divisive. I do this solely to communicate with speed and ease the CRT ideology.

CRT in the Culture and the Church

Critical theory ideology is a plague that has spread globally. From Marxist-driven arson and vandalism in Canada,[7] pastors arrested in the UK for "intolerance,"[8] DEI insanity in Australia,[9] to the colossal influence of Liberation Theology in Latin America.[10] But from here on out, we'll be looking at the specific infiltration of these Neo-Marxist ideas into the American culture and church. If you're thinking, "I don't think I remember seeing such inflammatory statements and ideas in our society," there's probably a couple of reasons for that. Most CRT ideas are coated with

---

6   For more answers like this see Bryan Osborne, *Quick Answers to Tough Questions* (Green Forest, AR: Master Books, 2017).

7   Cosmin Dzsurdzsa, "UPDATE: A map of the 100 churches that have been vandalized or burned since the residential schools announcement," True North, February 12, 2024, https://tnc. news/2024/02/12/a-map-of-every-church-burnt-or-vandalized-since-the-residential-school-announcements4/

8   Anugrah Kumar, "Judge to decide fate of British pastor facing prison for displaying Bible verse," *The Christian Post,* February 1, 2024, https://www.christianpost.com/news/british-pastor-facing-prison-for-displaying-bible-verse.html.

9   ABC News, "Thousands gather at Invasion Day rallies, calling for rethink of Australia Day," January 25, 2024, https://www.abc.net.au/news/2024-01-26/australia-day-invasion-day-dawn-service-rallies/103389696; The Christian Institute, Victoria's conversion therapy ban, https://www.christian.org.uk/wp-content/uploads/Briefing-Victorias-conversion-therapy-ban.pdf.

10 Declassified CIA document, "Liberation Theology: Religion, Reform, and Revolution," https://www.cia.gov/readingroom/docs/CIA-RDP97R00694R000600050001-9.pdf.

lofty language, written by academics for academics, and are originally tucked away in academic literature. This is not by accident. The primary venue for Marxist recruiting and training in America is the education system, especially college campuses. Those driven by Marxist philosophy have infiltrated, in mass, universities and colleges as professors and leadership. Their objective has been to train generations of our children to be Marxist revolutionaries, and they have been disastrously successful. The fruit of their efforts is manifest in so many ways by what is currently happening in our culture.

Also recognize that CRT goes under the cover of many different names, definitions, and phrases. That's why the rest of this book is so important. We'll be uncovering the key words, redefinitions, phrases, and actions that are slyly pushing the woke CRT agenda in every "nook and cranny" of American society. Sadly, this includes many churches and Christian institutions.

To hear "straight from the horse's mouth," I will quote often from the woke justice advocates whose words are exceptionally "illuminating." I will also be quoting many pastors and Christian leaders who have seemingly embraced various CRT ideas on some level. I will not spend a ton of time on them as that is not the goal of this book nor would it be in line with the succinct nature of this book. There will be links in the

Over half of church fires in the United States were caused by arson.

footnotes if you would like to research these Christian leaders and their teachings further. Please note, this is not an attempt to attack any of them personally. Nor is it the goal to dismiss their contribution to the church and apparent sincere desire for racial reconciliation. I am not arguing with their stated love for Christ, His Word, His bride, and the lost.

The purpose of these quotes, links, and references is to expose the infiltration of anti-biblical ideas into the body of Christ. Ideas that, whether these Christian leaders realize it or not, dramatically undermine biblical authority, biblical sufficiency, unity, actual reconciliation, and the gospel of Jesus Christ. It is imperative that the Christian be equipped to recognize and combat this subversive attack wherever it is found, but especially in the church.

5

Whiteness

Welcome to our first CRT buzzword, "Whiteness." In the CRT framework, this word has nothing to do with how clean your linens are and everything to do with assumed systemic oppression. Here is how the critical race theorists generally define and utilize this often slippery term.

Whiteness: 1. an ideology of assumed superiority created by, and for, whites; 2. this ideology is used to justify the oppression of non-whites; 3. used to create and sustain an oppressive "white dominant" culture; 4. anything that is part of "white culture" is systemically oppressive and racist

In 2020, the National Museum of African American History and Culture in Washington, D.C. created an infographic for their website to bring awareness to "whiteness." It was quickly removed after intense social backlash but can still be accessed from various online sources.[1] The infographic summarizes well many of the key aspects of "whiteness" according to CRT meaning. Here is their definition:

> "White dominant culture, or **whiteness**, refers to the way white people and their traditions, attitudes and ways of life have been normalized over time and are now considered standard practices in the United States. And since white people still hold most of the institutional power in America, we have all internalized some aspects of white culture — including people of color."[2]

1   Peggy McGlone, "African American Museum Site Removes 'Whiteness' Chart after Criticism from Trump Jr. and Conservative Media," *The Washington Post*, July 17, 2020, https://www.washingtonpost.com/entertainment/museums/african-american-museum-site-removes-whiteness-chart-after-criticism-from-trump-jr-and-conservative-media/2020/07/17/4ef6e6f2-c831-11ea-8ffe-372be8d82298_story.html.

2   Marina Watts, "Smithsonian Race Guidelines, Rational Thinking and Hard Work Are White Values," *Newsweek*, July 17, 2020, https://www.newsweek.com/smithsonian-race-guidelines-rational-thinking-hard-work-are-white-values-1518333.

It then goes on to identify 14 different categories that allegedly vibrantly display "whiteness" in America. They include, but are not limited to rugged individualism, family structure, emphasis on scientific method (logic), history (European focused), protestant work ethic, religion (Christianity as the norm), status-power-authority, future orientation, time (punctuality), aesthetics, holidays, justice, competition, and communication. It is not my intent to go over each one, but you'll notice that this list is a comprehensive summary of American society. Everything has been defined by "whiteness" because in CRT everything is oppressive.

Also, many of these things — family structure, scientific method, work ethic, Christianity as the norm, justice, etc. — come straight from a biblical worldview. Yet they're all viewed negatively as part of "whiteness" and branches of societal control exclusively benefitting whites. Again, CRT is not compatible with consistent Christianity.

So "whiteness" is the name given to the ideology that whites supposedly created to systemically oppress non-whites. This creed assumed the superiority of whites and allowed them to write the rules of society in accordance with their cultural practices. Thus, white cultural practices became dominant, normalized, and internalized, creating the hegemony and systemic oppression in America. Whiteness is only connected to white people, and anything that's a part of "white culture" is inherently tainted with CRT's lone sin of oppression.

It's important to note that "whiteness" is not considered a biological reality. It isn't that whites are actually better than blacks in any real way. Rather, it's considered a social reality because whites, as the oppressors, have imposed their fabricated superiority onto the culture for their advantage. Jarvis Williams, professor of NT studies at the Southern Baptist Theological Seminary and apparent sympathizer with portions of CRT, said it like this,

> "So then the question, is what is whiteness? Well here's something that's very important to realize, whiteness is not about your biology; it's about an ideology. It's a biological fiction but a social fact."[3]

This Christian professor at least embraces parts of the CRT narrative and defines "whiteness" as a fact. Not a biological fact but a social fact. It's worth reiterating that neither Scripture nor biology/genetics supports the idea of different races, which CRT hinges on. Every person has melanin, just various amounts, and melanin doesn't make anyone better or worse than anyone else. But for CRT, "whiteness" isn't about melanin but about social constructs.

So why is "whiteness" a "social fact" according to critical race theorists? Because of the oppressive white people who created it and the white people who sustain it, whether they realize it or not. White people today are either actively working to suppress black people, or they are benefitting from the repressive system which supports the oppression indirectly. Either way, only whites — and all whites — are responsible. CRT principally attaches all the cultural ills of American society to oppressive "whiteness" and white people. If your skin is light brown instead of dark brown, you're to blame.

As the plague of CRT thought has settled into our culture, institutions and corporations have been tripping all over themselves to appease the woke mob. That's why organizations like Coca-Cola® have been caught training their employees to be "less white." Not kidding. In 2021, an

---

3   For the New Christian Intellectual, Jarvis Williams on "Whiteness" Pursuing Gospel Centered Racial Reconciliation, YouTube, August 29, 2019, https://www.youtube.com/watch?v=TAYy3n-Ndy4Y.

employee leaked pictures of slides from online required training for
Coca-Cola® employees. Evidently, the curriculum being used was from
Robin DiAngelo, author of "White Fragility" and one of the primary
peddlers of CRT in America. From what was exposed, the corporate
training summarized the problem of "whiteness" and then let the
employees know how to "help." Answer: "Try to be less white."

"To be less white is to:
be less oppressive
be less arrogant
be less certain
be less defensive
be less ignorant
be more humble
listen [most likely to 'oppressed' voices]
believe
break with apathy
break with white solidarity"[4]

If you turn that around it means to be white is to be oppressive, arrogant,
certain, defensive, ignorant, prideful, dismissive, incredulous, apathetic,
complicit. A less than flattering view of white people. You get all this by
simply having less melanin. If you are born white, "whiteness" is inherent
to you, and you are prejudged as guilty. Black people, on the other hand,
cannot be guilty of things like arrogance and hatred, or anything else
negative, because they are the oppressed. In CRT, people are dubbed
innocent or guilty by virtue of skin shade alone. There's a word for
assuming superiority or inferiority about a person or group of people
based solely on a physical attribute like skin shade. Racism.[5]

4   Joel Abbott, "Coca-Cola® Holds 'Anti-racist' Training That Instructs Employees to 'BE
     LESS WHITE,' According to Whistleblower with Receipts," Not the Bee, February 20,
     2021, https://notthebee.com/article/coca-cola-holds-anti-racist-training-that-tells-employ-
     ees-be-less-white?fbclid=IwAR3-MUGpkqJI2pc_Ey_n3Vkd5SroLIHpuQINIIYcOoz077yHbU-
     R8O6tB7rM.

5   I use this term for its familiarity. Ethnic prejudice or partiality is a better biblical definition.
     https://answersingenesis.org/racism/what-really-separates-us/.

As mentioned earlier, this racist ideology dominates America's educational institutions. Just do a quick Google search and you'll find an endless catalog of college courses dealing with the problem of "whiteness." But it is no longer confined to the realms of higher learning, it has crawled all the way down to elementary education. Imagine the impact this is having on students as they're being taught by teachers and administrators that they're innocent or guilty because of their skin. For instance, it was reported in July of 2021 that at least 25 public school districts in 12 states were teaching a book entitled, *Not My Idea: A Book about Whiteness.*[6] It was being taught to multiple grade levels including elementary students. It was also reported that many private schools, libraries, and even churches used or promoted the book in some way. The book seems to have slyly covered CRT's highlights in a "child friendly" format.

This "children's book" essentially informs kids they are fighting against oppression and whiteness for their own liberation. That "White supremacy has been lying to kids for centuries." At one point in the book, the main character is offered a contract by a demonic-like figure to sign up for whiteness. According to the contract, if the character agrees, they get "stolen land, stolen riches," and "special favors." And "whiteness" gets "to

6   Sam Dorman, "At Least 25 Public Schools, Districts Pushing Kids' Book Featuring 'Whiteness' Contract with Devil: Report," Fox News, July 8, 2021, https://www.foxnews.com/us/school-districts-whiteness-contract-book.

mess endlessly with the lives of your friends, neighbors, loved ones, and all fellow humans of COLOR." Oh, and "whiteness" also gets "your soul."[7] Imagine kids 5–10 years old being told they are automatically signed up for a deal with the devil based on the shade of their skin. Imagine it's your child. Depending on where they go to school, it might be.

Also, arguing that certain cultural characteristics like work ethic, nuclear family, emphasis on logic, etc. are wrong because they're "white" is to be ignorant — ignorant of both reality and history. Many other cultures, both present and past, possess values similar to America's — cultures predominantly light brown, cultures predominantly dark brown, and everything in between. Yes, America was founded by mainly white people with a general inclination to certain cultural values. But what makes a cultural value right or wrong isn't the amount of melanin in the skin of the people who established it. Nor does the value's pervasiveness within a culture determine its worth. A cultural value is right or wrong based solely on its alignment with God's flawless values and commands located in His Word.

> The law of the Lord is perfect, reviving the soul; the
> testimony of the Lord is sure, making wise the simple
> (Psalm 19:7).

> Whoever has my commandments and keeps them, he it is
> who loves me (John 14:21).

God's Word is the source of everlasting perfect truth. God defines what practices are wise and foolish, good and evil. The ideas of mankind, no matter their skin shade, do not.

As should be readily apparent, the idea of "whiteness" stands in direct contradiction to the Bible. Attaching innate evil to everything "white" and white people merely because of their skin shade is a gross display of the sin of prejudice and partiality. Scripture tells us,

---

7   Anastasia Higginbotham, *Not My Idea: A Book about Whiteness* (New York, NY: Dottir Press, 2018).

*You shall not be partial in judgment. You shall hear the
small and the great alike. You shall not be intimidated by
anyone, for the judgment is God's (Deuteronomy 1:17).*

*So Peter opened his mouth and said: "Truly I understand
that God shows no partiality, but in every nation anyone
who fears him and does what is right is acceptable to him"
(Acts 10:34–35).*

The idea of "whiteness" is entirely anti-biblical and sinisterly divisive.

CRT declares that "whiteness" is the cause of society's evils past and
present. Jarvis Williams, the seminary professor mentioned earlier, said
this after asserting "whiteness" is a social fact,

"One reason we get slavery is because of the construct of whiteness."[8]

Based on the context of this video and his other teachings, I would
venture to say he believes it's the primary reason for slavery. Sadly, this is
in lock step with CRT dogma. The evils America experiences, historically
and presently, come from "whiteness" and the white people who created

Old Rock House in Alton, Illinois, a historical symbol of solidarity where whites aided African
Americans escaping the horrors of slavery.

---

8   For the New Christian Intellectual, Jarvis Williams on "Whiteness" Pursuing Gospel Centered Racial
    Reconciliation, YouTube, August 29, 2019, https://www.youtube.com/watch?v=TAYy3nNdy4Y.

and perpetuate it. In CRT the problem isn't sin, common to all humanity, it's skin.

This could not be more disconnected from biblical truth and thus reality. The Bible explicitly pronounces that all are sinners. Evil is not limited to one shade of skin.

> As it is written: "None is righteous, no, not one; no one understands; no one seeks for God. All have turned aside; together they have become worthless; no one does good, not even one" (Romans 3:10–12).

We get slavery because of sin, not skin. This is why slavery is seen throughout human history, everywhere in the world, long before the construct of "whiteness." By no means are the evils of prejudice and slavery unique to America. What is unique to America, and other places like Great Britain, is the way slavery was abolished and prejudice progressively condemned. These movements came at great cost and are historically unheard of.

What drove these movements against the strong current of global historical precedence? The biblical worldview that demands recognition and submission to God's truth that every human is endowed by their Creator with equal intrinsic worth. The cruel ethnic-based slavery that previously plagued America and the west is wholly denounced by God's Word![9] Slave traders ("kidnappers/men stealers") are among the worst of sinners listed in 1 Timothy 1:10. Exodus 21:16 states,

> He who kidnaps a man, whether he sells him or he is found in his possession, shall surely be put to death (NASB).

Numerous historians credit Christian thought and deed for the abolition of slavery in most countries. The cause for slavery in America wasn't "whiteness," it was sin. The solution for that slavery wasn't a Marxist revolution, it was God's Word rightly applied. CRT gets the core problems

---

9   For more on this, https://answersingenesis.org/bible-questions/doesnt-the-bible-support-slavery/.

William Wilberforce tirelessly campaigned to end slavery in the British Empire, dedicating his life to abolition and securing the passage of the Slave Trade Act of 1807.

— and solutions — of the past, present, and future incredibly wrong. Not surprising since it's based on man's fallible, finite, Marxist ideas. But obedience to God's Word always has been and always will be the answer to the problems we face.

It's also worth mentioning, there have been many other times in history where a society has broadly blamed all its problems on one group of people. It never ends well. To demonize a group of people for the shade of their skin is the very definition of injustice. But this is woke justice.

6

White Privilege

In the ideological world of Critical Race Theory, "whiteness" permeates and produces "white privilege." Recall that the goal of "whiteness" was to oppress non-whites for the benefit of the white oppressors. White Privilege is an all-inclusive title that encompasses all the advantages the oppressors unjustly receive. Here is a concise definition:

White Privilege: 1. Unearned advantages possessed by whites in a society created by and for whites. 2. Whiteness was established to create and entrench white privilege.

For a longer explanation of white privilege, I turn to its initial popularizer, woke scholar and activist Peggy McIntosh. In her paper "White Privilege: Unpacking the invisible Knapsack," she defines white privilege this way:

> "I have come to see white privilege as an invisible package of unearned assets that I can count on cashing in each day, but about which I was "meant" to remain oblivious. White privilege is like an invisible weightless knapsack of special provisions, maps, passports, code books, visas, clothes, tools, and blank checks."[1]

This collection of "assets" and "special provisions" known as white privilege, is unearned because it is purely the consequence of the unjust systemic oppression of whiteness. It is invisible because of the foundational CRT tenet that racist oppression "is engrained in the fabric and system of the American society."[2] The oppression is so engrained and normalized that people, oppressed and oppressor alike, can't see it unless there is an intervention to awaken them to the truth.

1   Peggy McIntosh, "White Privilege: Unpacking the Invisible Knapsack," https://www.wcwonline.org/images/pdf/Knapsack_plus_Notes-Peggy_McIntosh.pdf.
2   "What Is Critical Race Theory?" UCLA School of Public Affairs, Critical Race Studies, http://spacrs.wordpress.com/what-is-critical-race-theory.

This goes back to the idea of hegemony discussed earlier. In my obviously "fictitious" example, my daughter Macie assumes that losing Ian's game every time is normal because that's all she's experienced. But what if my son Ian learned the game, with all its biased rules, from his father? Who designed the game so that the guys always win? As Ian plays the game with Macie and wins each time, his experience will teach him that winning is only natural. He'll believe it's natural because that's all he knows, and he is ignorant of how rigged the rules are in his favor. Though his advantage, or privilege if you will, is invisible to both him and Macie, it remains just the same.

According to CRT, this is how white privilege remains invisible and flies under the cultural radar.

The oppression, with its privileges afforded to the oppressors, has been so thoroughly normalized over generations that people have internalized its reality. As a result, no one, oppressor or oppressed, sees the oppressor's advantages as abnormal.

Notice that the "invisible weightless knapsack" of white privilege contains assets to benefit whites in every realm of life. This connects back to CRT's core belief that any disparity in outcome between oppressor and oppressed is the result of — and evidence for — discriminatory oppression. The sole reason any white person would achieve more than

a black person is because of the benefits — the white privilege — that whiteness, systemic racism, provides. It is for this same reason that any black person would be less successful by comparison. The weight of systemic oppression coupled with the unfair assistance of white privilege to whites is too much to overcome. If there is any disparity in outcome between whites and blacks, CRT pronounces systemic racism as the cause and effect. As mentioned earlier, things like habits, choices, character, abilities, opportunities, etc. are irrelevant. The conclusive issue is whether your skin is black or white. Through the oppression of whiteness and the advantage of white privilege, whites have acquired a disproportionate amount of wealth and power in America.

By this illicit gain, whites have stolen from blacks, and thus the absolute necessity for reparations in both resources and cultural influence.

At this point it's worth reminding ourselves that CRT, as a worldview, assumes all these things before sincerely looking at the culture. To bring this fact back into focus, check out this quote from Robin DiAngelo, "high priestess" of CRT,

> "Whiteness Studies begin with the premise that racism and white privilege exist in both traditional and modern forms, and rather than work to prove its existence, work to reveal it."[3]

CRT is not working to prove systemic racism, whiteness, and white privilege; it's working to find in the culture what it "knows," assumes, is already there. It puts on "whiteness glasses," looks at society, and lo and behold, sees whiteness and white privilege everywhere. Of course it does, how could it not?

But honestly, it's not surprising (though still highly problematic for the culture) that secularists are assuming and applying faulty secular assumptions. The much larger problem is that many Christians, Christian leaders, and pastors are buying into those same assumptions. For example, Matt Chandler, the highly influential senior pastor of the

---

3   Robin DiAngelo, *International Journal of Critical Pedagogy*, Vol 3 (3) (2011) p. 56, https://libjournal.uncg.edu/ijcp/article/viewFile/249/116.

Village Church based in Flower Mound, Texas, made a video specifically addressing white privilege. In it he said this:

> "I have grown up with this invisible kind of bag of privilege, this kind of invisible toolkit, that I can reach in there at any given moment and have this type of privilege that a lot of other brothers and sisters don't have … and so if I could just kind of lay it all out there what I'm talking about right now is white privilege."[4]

It literally sounds like he just "copied and pasted" Peggy McIntosh's definition for white privilege. He gives and wholly affirms the same basic definition with a glaze of "Christianese."

To be clear, Pastor Chandler doesn't seem to fully embrace CRT. Maybe he could be called "CRT-lite"? I'm also not questioning his love for God or what appears to be a deep desire for racial reconciliation.[5] It seems he genuinely believes that this understanding of white privilege is key to moving the needle toward unity. And that's the problem. He's importing into his church an idea that literally comes from an anti-biblical worldview that fundamentally views Christianity itself as part of the oppressive problem. In the name of unity, he's encouraging Christians to embrace an ideology whose sole purpose is to bring about strife, division, and destruction. Unbeknownst to him, he has swallowed — and is prescribing — a poisonous idea that undermines the very unity and reconciliation he so passionately wants. Pastor Chandler may have the best motivations, but if you ingest a poison, even with the best of intent, it will bring harm and death, nonetheless.

Whether he realizes it or not, he's essentially assumed — and is teaching — that the biblical worldview isn't enough to understand and deal with racial reconciliation. The Bible, the Word of God, is insufficient, and

---

4   Interestingly, but not surprisingly, the original video has been removed from the church You-Tube page. Here's a link that shows a good portion of his original video: https://www.youtube.com/watch?v=UuYtk38q5XA&t=32s. And here is a link to my presentation on CRT that shows part of Chandler's original video (start at 25:14): https://www.youtube.com/watch?v=GeYJI-Jfh2MY&t=1514s.

5   Like with the word "racism," I use "racial reconciliation" for its familiarity. But since there is only one race and multiple ethnicities, "ethnic reconciliation" is much more accurate.

we need outside help. But really? God's Word isn't enough? We need help from an anti-Christian pagan religion to diagnose this societal problem and, in turn, aid in prescribing the solution? Importing beliefs and practices from paganism never worked out well for Israel in the Old Testament and it won't end well for the church today.

Unfortunately, Chandler is far from alone. Prominent pastor, author, and co-founder of the Gospel Coalition, Tim Keller, who is now in glory, had this to say on the issue of white privilege during a panel discussion (fixed with bold):

"A friend of mine, recently, who's a pastor, was talking to a Norwegian man.... And at one point he heard the pastor talking about the fact that we [whites] were all complicit.... Afterwards, the white, the Norwegian came up and said, 'No, no, no, I'm Norwegian. No. Had nothing to do with it.' And my pastor friend said, 'Studies have shown … that if you have **white skin**, it's worth a million dollars over a lifetime over somebody who doesn't have white skin. And that's because of historical forces' … as I mentioned: if you have that **asset** of **white skin** right now … then you actually **have to say**, 'I didn't deserve this.' And also, to some degree, 'I'm the product of and standing on the shoulders of other people who got that through injustice.' So,

the Bible actually says, yes, **you** are **involved in injustice**. And even if you didn't actually do it ... **You're part of the problem.**"[6]

In a nutshell, white skin is an unjust "asset" that gives unearned benefits: white privilege.[7] Notice that all that matters is "white skin." It doesn't matter if your family just moved to America from Norway. It doesn't matter if your white family grew up poor and is still penniless today. It doesn't matter if your direct ancestors were slaves, never owned a slave, or were directly responsible for the abolition of slavery. According to Pastor Keller, if you have the unearned "asset" of white skin, "you are involved in injustice" by definition. If you are white, you are inherently "part of the problem." This could not be more racist.

Although this line of reasoning is fully in line with CRT philosophy, it is in direct conflict with Scripture. What's being proposed is some form of "generational" or "ancestral" guilt. That whites today are guilty because of the sins of past whites. But the Bible unequivocally and repeatedly states that each person dies for their own sins.

---

6   Woke Preacher Clips, Tim Keller: "If You Have White Skin, It's Worth $1 Million Over A Life-time," YouTube, September 21, 2020, https://www.youtube.com/watch?v=qiXDvQzlS1c.

7   For a good discussion about whether or not "white privilege" is the best conclusion to jump to for explaining discrepancies among ethnic groups, I encourage reading chapter 8 of *Fault Lines* by Voddie Baucham.

*Behold, all souls are mine; the soul of the father as well
as the soul of the son is mine: **the soul who sins shall die**
(Ezekiel 18:4, emphasis mine).*

*Fathers shall not be put to death because of their children,
nor shall children be put to death because of their fathers.
But each one shall die for his own sin
(2 Kings 14:6, emphasis mine).*

God's Word lets us know that we're not guilty of, nor condemned for, the sins of our ancestors (or those who simply share a similar skin shade). Each individual is responsible for their own sins for which they will give an account (Romans 14:12). We are guilty because of our own sins, and we die because of our own sins. The idea of guilt by association or generational guilt is completely contrary to God's Word and is derived solely from the minds of men.[8]

Pastor Keller's sentiments reflect the thoughts and teachings of so many influential voices in Christianity today. Professing believers who have been seduced by aspects of CRT, if not the whole ideology. An ideology that assigns guilt based on melanin, rejects biblical authority, and inevitably leads to a false works-based gospel. Those advocating these ideas may have good intentions, but you can have the best of intentions and end up with the worst of consequences.

---

8   In an attempt to prove "generational guilt" is biblical, some point to passages like Exodus 20:5, "You shall not bow down to them or worship them; for I, the Lord your God, am a jealous God, punishing the children for the sin of the fathers to the third and fourth generation of those who hate me." But when taken in context, this verse, and others like it, is not saying that children are guilty because of the sins committed by their fathers. Rather, children tend to practice the sins of parents. And as children repeat the sins of the previous generation they too will be rightly punished. It is also referring to the reality the children suffer from the consequences of their parent's sins. Although children are not guilty of the sins of their parents, they are profoundly impacted by them.

7

White Supremacy

Whatever pops into your head when you think of white supremacy is likely wrong according to CRT advocates. Or, at the very least, drastically insufficient. The idea of white supremacy only being related to burning crosses, the KKK, or the Nazis is antiquated and a scapegoat for America's oppressors. Critical race theorists dynamically redefine this loaded title to establish and announce the guilt of all the members of the oppressive white identity group. What is white supremacy according to CRT? Voddie Baucham, in his outstanding book *Fault Lines*, provides a clear explanation:

> "White Supremacy: any belief, behavior, or system that supports, promotes, or enhances white privilege."[1]

According to CRT, since whiteness made America systemically oppressive, everything in America "supports, promotes, or enhances white privilege." Therefore, America is defined by white supremacy. In case you're getting dizzy from all the terms, ideas, and "white" talk, let me summarize. The ideology of whiteness (white superiority) creates white privilege, white privilege entrenches systemic oppression — white supremacy, white supremacy leads to continued white privilege. The cycle of white privilege and white supremacy, established by whiteness, is perpetual. All in all, white supremacy (redefined) is another name for CRT's assumed systemic oppression of blacks by whites.

CRT dealers Robin DiAngelo and Ozlem Sensoy, in their award-winning textbook, *Is Everyone Really Equal?* help us understand CRT's meaning of white supremacy:

---

1   Voddie Baucham, *Fault Lines: The Social Justice Movement and Evangelicalism's Looming Catastrophe* (New York, NY: Salem Books, 2021), p. 74.

"When we use the term White supremacy, we are not referring to extreme hate groups or 'bad racists.' We use the term to capture the all-encompassing dimensions of White privilege, dominance, and assumed superiority [whiteness] in mainstream society."[2]

White supremacy no longer refers to "extreme hate groups," which would reflect its actual long-term definition. White supremacy now signifies the sinister oppression found in all "mainstream society." There are not just "bad racists" anymore because all whites, as oppressors, are racist regardless of their attitudes, words, or deeds. White supremacy is described as "all-encompassing," indicating that it's systemic, happening everywhere all the time. It is the cultural water we swim in, and whites built the aquarium and filled it with water suited for them. If you're white, the water is great for you. If you're black, the water is toxic. Unless a new aquarium is built, filled with new water, white supremacy with its privileged whites will reign supreme.

Please understand, critical race theory states that all whites benefit from the system, thus support the system, consequently they're all part of white supremacy. All whites are participating in white supremacy (knowingly or

Tamir Rice, a 12-year-old African American boy, was tragically killed by police while playing with a toy gun, igniting widespread protests.

---

2   Robin DiAngelo and Ozlem Sensoy, *Is Everyone Really Equal? An Introduction to Key Concepts in Social Justice Education* (Second Edition, Multicultural Education Series) (New York, NY: Teachers college Press, 2017), p. 143.

ignorantly), all whites are white supremacists. The title white supremacist is no longer reserved for someone in a white hood or sporting a weird mustache. The teacher, policeman, pastor, architect, soccer mom, athlete, movie star, grandparent, accountant, first grader, everyone — if they are white — is a white supremacist. Remember, it is the asset of white skin alone that condemns a person as "part of the problem."

This redefinition of white supremacy is inflammatory, accusatory, divisive, and diabolical. We should expect no less from a Marxist ideology whose sole purpose is to divide, conquer, and rebuild a society. And since CRT is a worldview, just a quick internet search reveals woke neo-Marxist advocates are "seeing" white supremacy everywhere. Here's just a sampling of the types of headlines you'll find:

≫ **"Woke Educators Declare Objective Math White Supremacy."**[3]
That's right — even math is racist.

≫ **"Denial of Evolution Is a Form of White Supremacy"**[4]
"Evolution denial … is a form of white supremacy that perpetuates segregation and violence against Black bodies."

≫ **"Crazy people: Trying to stop the wholesale abortion of black babies is 'intrinsically tied to white supremacy'"**[5]
"The anti-choice movement is intrinsically tied to white supremacy. White men want power and control, and Black folks controlling their reproductive lives threatens their racist worldview."

---

3   Kerry McDonald, "Woke Educators Declare Objective Math White Supremacy," Catalyst, March 15, 2021, https://catalyst.independent.org/2021/03/15/woke-educators-math-white-supremacy/.

4   Allison Hopper, "Denial of Evolution Is a Form of White Supremacy," *Scientific American*, July 5, 2021, https://www.scientificamerican.com/article/denial-of-evolution-is-a-form-of-white-supremacy/.

5   Joel Abbott, Crazy people: Trying to stop the wholesale abortion of black babies is 'intrinsically tied to white supremacy,'" Not the Bee, February 28, 2021, https://notthebee.com/article/crazy-people-trying-to-stop-the-slaughter-of-black-babies-is-intrinsically-tied-to-white-supremacy.

≫ **"Why Waking Up Early Is Rooted in White Supremacy"**[6]
Recall that a strong work ethic geared toward success is a product of whiteness.

≫ **"Scientists rename birds to 'shun racism,' defeat white supremacy."**[7]
I have no words.

I could go on, but you get the idea. Of course, it almost goes without saying that CRT has flooded higher academia with countless courses on whiteness/white supremacy available on college campuses nationwide. And as alluded to in a previous chapter, that ideology is seeping to the earliest levels of education. Consider also that the vast majority of DEI — Diversity, Equity, Inclusion — training for federal employees and private corporations is unquestionably saturated with critical race theory. We saw an example of this earlier when examining the employee training of corporate giant Coca-Cola®, and its admonition to its employees to be "less white." Check out this headline about employee training for another corporate giant, "Walmart to workers: You're racists: Training program claims U.S. a 'white supremacy system.'"[8] According to the article, Walmart has been caught training its employees that:

> "Whites are inherently racist and the United States is a 'white supremacy system' designed by white Europeans 'for the purpose of assigning and maintaining white skin access to power and privilege.'"

> "Colonists constructed a 'white race' in 1680 that has led to white Americans undergoing 'racist conditioning' that indoctrinates them into 'white supremacy.'"

---

6   Not the Bee, "Why Waking Up Early Is Rooted in White Supremacy," May 22, 2023, https://notthebee.com/article/why-waking-up-early-is-rooted-in-white-supremacy.

7   Not the Bee, "Scientists rename birds to 'shun racism,' defeat white supremacy," November 1, 2023, https://notthebee.com/article/were-renaming-dozens-of-species-of-birds-now-because-everything-is-racist.

8   Art Moore, "Walmart to workers: You're racists: Training program claims U.S. a 'white supremacy system,' "*WND*, October 14, 2021, https://www.wnd.com/2021/10/4952883/.

White Supremacy

"Whites, according to the trainers, are inherently guilty of 'white privilege' and 'internalized racial superiority.'"[9]

"Whites must accept the idea that 'white is not right' and acknowledge their guilt and shame."

Walmart's CRT training proclaims that if you're white, you're guilty of white supremacy, white privilege, and racism; and you must bear your shame. Based on skin shade alone, whites are assigned the revolting titles of white supremacist and racist. This could not be more racist. Virgil Walker from G3 and Just Thinking Ministries has rightly said, "CRT is culturally acceptable racism."[10] I would extend that sentiment one step further and suggest that CRT is culturally celebrated racism. But celebrated or not, racism is always wrong, whenever it occurs, to whomever it occurs. A notable leader of the civil rights movement, Martin Luther King Jr., expressed a powerful vision for the future—a hope that his children would one day live in a nation where people are evaluated based on their character rather than their skin color. One must wonder what happened to that grand desire.[11]

CRT literally judges people by the color of their skin. This subversive idea profoundly contradicts the Bible and the foundational driving idea of the civil rights movement.

But perhaps most disturbing, this new neo-Marxist understanding of white supremacy is invading Christian thought. Daniel Hill, founding pastor of River City Community Church in Illinois and author of *White Awake*, writes this in his book,

---

9   This quote comes from another article on the same training program. It also contains a link to the actual training documents if you would like to read them for yourself. Christopher F. Rufo, "Walmart Vs. Whiteness," *City Journal*, October 14, 2021, https://www.city-journal.org/article/walmart-vs-whiteness.

10   Virgil L. Walker, Executive Director of Operations for G3 Ministries and co-host of the Just Thinking Podcast, https://justthinking.me/ep-108-critical-race-theory/.

11   Martin Luther King Jr. Speech at Civil Rights March, Washington, D.C., August 28, 1963.

"I repent all the time because I believe I'm surrounded by the sickness of racism. I see the sickness in the ideology of white supremacy and have no doubt that it has infected me."[12]

I think it's safe to say that when Pastor Hill says he's been "infected" with white supremacy it does not mean he has a strange desire to join the KKK. He has embraced CRT thinking and its new prejudicial definition of white supremacy.

Christina Barland Edmondson, a higher education instructor and author of *Faithful Antiracism,* wrote an article for *Christianity Today* entitled "The Shocking Necessity of Racist Violence." In it she said this,

"White supremacy's sinful dance, swaying back and forth between Klansmen's sheets and clergy robes, pains and plagues Christian[s] of color and lies to white Christians…. White Christianity's very design exists to maintain false piety and sear the consciences of white people against the oppression and exploitation of blacks."[13]

When she says "white Christianity," is she referring to all white Christians around the globe? Of course not. Only white Christians in America have

12 Daniel Hill, *White Awake: An Honest Look at What It Means to Be White* (Downers Grove, IL: IVP Books, 2017), p. 139.

13 Christina Barland Edmondson, "The Shocking Necessity of Racist Violence," *Christianity Today,* October 9, 2020, https://www.christianitytoday.com/ct/2020/october-web-only/shocking-ne-cessity-of-racist-violence.html.

had their consciences seared. Effectively, white Christians can't or won't see the oppression of blacks because the structure of "white Christianity" is an extension of whiteness and white supremacy.

Notice the division CRT brings with it into the church — oppressive white Christianity versus oppressed black Christianity, victimized Black Christians versus privileged white Christians. When you bring CRT into Christianity, by its very nature it demands a distinction be made between whites and blacks within the body of Christ. But God says,

> *for in Christ Jesus you are all sons of God, through faith.*
> *For as many of you as were baptized into Christ have put*
> *on Christ. There is neither Jew nor Greek, there is neither*
> *slave nor free, there is no male and female, for you are all*
> *one in Christ Jesus (Galatians 3:26–28).*

CRT unapologetically, and purposefully, seeks to forcibly obliterate the innate unity of Christianity. Christians need to wake up to this and reject CRT for the divisive pagan philosophy that it is.

Now consider Matthew Hall, former provost of Southern Baptist Theological Seminary. During his time there he told white Christians that their traditional Christian faith, upbringing, and worldview is basically one big lie. That what looks like a "beautiful narrative of faithfulness and orthodoxy, and of truth and righteousness and justice" is established on the "rotting corpse of white supremacy."[14]

Echoing this sentiment, Jamar Tisby, author of *Color of Compromise* and leading evangelical woke voice, said this in a column for the *New York Times,*

> "White Christians have to face the possibility that everything they
> have learned about how to practice their faith has been designed to
> explicitly or implicitly reinforce a racist structure."[15]

---

14 Reformation Charlotte, Matthew Hall — Rotting Corpse of White Supremacy, YouTube, November 5, 2021, https://www.youtube.com/watch?v=3cBl_5wELVs.

15 Jamar Tisby, "Is the White Church Inherently Racist?" *The New York Times,* August 18, 2020, https://www.nytimes.com/2020/08/18/books/review/white-too-long-robert-p-jones.html.

These voices in Christian spaces are parroting the CRT narrative that says if you're white, everything you assumed was normal and true in this world is a mirage. Your Christian faith and traditions aren't good, they're vile because they're drenched in white supremacy, and so are you. You, white Christian, are inherently a racist, white supremacist. But assigning someone the awful label of white supremacist based solely on the amount of melanin in their skin is the literal definition of racism! It's the sin of ethnic partiality (James 2:9). It's also bearing false witness and slander — all of which Scripture strictly forbids.

> *You shall not bear false witness against your neighbor*
> *(Exodus 20:16).*

> *Brothers and sisters, do not slander one another*
> *(James 4:11; NIV).*

Ironically, CRT fully contradicts the dream of Martin Luther King Jr. that all people should be judged by the content of their character. Infinitely more important, it repetitively and egregiously violates God's law. Far from being a helpful tool for reconciliation, CRT creates and fuels hostility. Critical race theory breeds racism. And racism is always wrong, whenever it occurs, to whomever it occurs. But critical race theorists have found a way around this. To find out how, let's look at what CRT does with the definition of racism.

8

Racism Redefined

As with white supremacy, CRT gives the meaning of racism a complete overhaul. If you look up the definition for racism in the Merriam-Webster dictionary this is what you'll find:

> "a belief that race is a fundamental determinant of human traits and capacities and that racial differences produce an inherent superiority of a particular race."[1]

The belief that some races (people groups) are innately superior to others has been the dominant understanding of racism for over 100 years. It is this definition of racism that accurately describes people like Charles Darwin, Adolf Hitler, and Karl Marx. Darwin predicted in his book *The Descent of Man,*

> "At some future period … the civilized races of man will almost certainly exterminate and replace the savage races throughout the world."[2]

Darwin decreed the civilized races to be those with light skin (like himself), and the savage races were those with dark skin. Of course, racism did not originate with evolution. The origin of racism is sin. But what Darwin's hypothesis did was throw gas on the fire of the sin of racism. It gave some people, in their minds, a "scientific justification" for their racism. This is clearly seen in Hitler, who was recorded saying,

> "Should I not also have the right to eliminate millions of an inferior race that multiplies like vermin?"[3]

---

1   https://www.merriam-webster.com/dictionary/racism.

2   Charles Darwin, *The Descent of Man* (Chicago, IL: William Benton in Great Books of the Western World, 1952), p. 336.

3   Adolf Hitler, quoted in *Hitler*, by Joachim Fest (Vintage Books Edition, 1974), p. 679–680.

This sort of evolutionary driven racism is also seen in statements from Karl Marx. In a letter he wrote to Friedrich Engels, he endorsed Pierre Trémaux's evolutionary book *Origin and Transformations of Man and Other Beings* (originally in French). Marx said this about the book:

> "its historical and political applications far more significant and pregnant than Darwin .... [Trémaux] shows that the common negro type is only a degeneration of a far higher one."[4]

This is racism. Or at least it was. According to critical race theorists, that definition of racism is outdated, insufficient, misinformed, and obsolete. Here is the critical theorist's enlightened redefinition:

Racism: Systemic, institutional, and corporate bias that advantages one group (whites).

Racism is no longer primarily about an individual's beliefs, attitudes, words, or actions. It has evolved into a corporate system of thought and practice that's been infused into all of society that advantages and empowers the white oppressors. Ibram X. Kendi, author of *New York Times* bestseller *How to Be an Antiracist* and CRT rockstar, defines racism this way,

> "Racism is a marriage of racist policies and racist ideas that produces and normalizes racial inequities.... Racism itself is institutional, structural, and systemic."[5]

Alicia Garza, co-founder of Black Lives Matter (an organization of "trained Marxists"[6] according to Patrisse Cullors, another BLM co-founder), offers a similar definition,

---

4   Karl Marx, in a letter to Friedrich Engels dated August 7, 1866, available in *Karl Marx and Friedrich Engels: Collected Works,* Volume 42 [1864–1868], trans. Christopher Upward and John Peet [New York, NY: International Publishers; Moscow: Progress Publishers, 1987], p. 305, https://archive.org/details/karlmarxfrederic0042marx/mode/2up?q=%22far+higher+one%22.

5   Ibram X. Kendi, *How to Be an Antiracist* (New York, NY: Random House Publishing Group, 2019), p. 17–18.

6   Yaron Steinbuch, "Black Lives Matter Co-founder Describes Herself as 'Trained Marxist,'" *New York Post*, June 25, 2020, https://nypost.com/2020/06/25/blm-co-founder-describes-herself-as-trained-marxist/.

Laws and lawmakers are considered a fallible part of the broken system of justice.

"I'm also going to talk about racism and what it really is. Because oftentimes we talk about it as if its people being mean to each other. When in fact it, they [racism] are systems that are backed by power that impact the outcomes of people's lives."[7]

Recall back in chapter two that the UCLA Luskin School of Public Affairs outlined racism this way within the CRT paradigm,

"CRT recognizes that racism is engrained in the fabric and system of the American society. The individual racist need not exist to note that institutional racism is pervasive in the dominant culture."[8]

Amazingly, in CRT, racists aren't even required for racism. Its intrinsically imbedded in the very system of the United States. And you can see the sizable influence of CRT thinking in our culture by looking at Merriam-Webster's secondary definition for racism,

---

7 KPBS Public Media, A Conversation With Black Lives Matter Co-Founder Alicia Garza, YouTube, February 27, 2015, https://www.youtube.com/watch?v=4J02x0pLMZ4.

8 "What Is Critical Race Theory?" UCLA Luskin School of Public Affairs, Critical Race Studies, http://spacrs.wordpress.com/what-is-critical-race-theory.

"the systemic oppression of a racial group to the social, economic, and political advantage of another [-] specifically: WHITE SUPREMACY"[9]

Note the repeated emphasis on system and systemic. Racism, according to CRT, is corporate, not individual. It is everywhere, in everything, and it is happening all the time. CRT guru Robin DiAngelo had this to say about the regularity of racism in a handout on the subject,

> "The question is not 'did racism take place'? but rather 'how did racism manifest in that situation?'"[10]

You're not allowed to ask if racism occurred, only how. Why? Because CRT is a biased worldview that is unfalsifiable. It assumes racism is systemic and then sees it in every societal structure, institution, and situation. Take this scenario, for example. Two people walk into a store, one white and one black. If the store clerk goes to help the white customer, CRT says it's because the clerk assigns higher value to the white customer. If the clerk goes over to the black customer, it's because she doesn't trust the customer with more melanin to be left alone. Either way, no matter what the clerk does, CRT cries racism. I like how Darrell Harrison, pastor and co-host of the superb *Just Thinking* podcast, put it, "Critical race theorists see the entire world through 'race colored' glasses."[11] In CRT, everything is racist.

The CRT propaganda of systemic racism has shown up in numerous ways in our culture. In 2021, a large school system in Maryland was fervently informing their students that "A 'Dual Pandemic' — COVID-19 And 'Systemic Racism'"[12] was taking place. The American Psychological Associa-

---

9 https://www.merriam-webster.com/dictionary/racism.

10 https://robindiangelo.com/wp-content/uploads/2016/06/Anti-racism-handout-1-page-2016.pdf.

11 Darrell Harrison, "Episode 108 Critical Race Theory," *Just Thinking* Podcast, February 23, 2021, https://justthinking.me/ep-108-critical-race-theory/.

12 Kendall Tietz, "Maryland School System Told Students There Is a 'Dual Pandemic' — COVID-19 And 'Systemic Racism,'" *Tampa Free Press*, November 5, 2021, https://www.tampafp.com/maryland-school-system-told-students-there-is-a-dual-pandemic-covid-19-and-systemic-racism/.

tion has asserted in the past that "We Are Living in a Racism Pandemic."[13] The dogma of systemic racism is fundamental to the CRT movement. Yet if systemic racism is indeed a reality, how can the "oppressed" call out their "oppressors" and not get demolished? The fact that the "revolt" of the oppressed is allowed, and even culturally applauded, could be argued as significant evidence against systemic racism. Virgil Walker from Just Thinking ministries, powerfully makes this case,

> "Only in a first world country like America does CRT have the chance to flourish. Only in a nation bent on writing historical wrongs can CRT find fertile ground. Only in a country devoid of systemic racism can you find people able to cry systemic racism and not be crushed by the same system they claim is racist."[14]

Nonetheless, CRT activists assume that racism is in America's DNA because it is considered America's original sin. The slavery and prejudice in America's past reveal racism as its core systemic problem. That's why critical race theory is applied to America. This original sin started with the first whites who created and instituted whiteness to oppress blacks for white benefit. That sin was then passed on to all subsequent whites, all of whom benefitted from America's oppressive systemic racism regardless of intentions. By profiting from racism, all whites are sustaining racism directly or indirectly, therefore all whites are racists. By now you probably saw that conclusion coming. It's still the anti-biblical idea of imputed or generational guilt (2 Kings 14:6). It's still the sins of partiality, bearing false witness, and slander (James 2:9, Deuteronomy 5:20, Exodus 23:1). CRT effectively says an entire group of people, whites, are inherently inferior solely because of a physical trait: skin shade. This is the very definition of racism and in alignment with Darwin, Hitler, Marx, and the KKK. Talk about bad company.

---

13 American Psychological Association, "We Are Living in a Racism Pandemic," Says APA President, Press release, May 29, 2020, https://www.apa.org/news/press/releases/2020/05/racism-pandemic.

14 Virgil Walker, Episode 108 Critical Race Theory, *Just Thinking* Podcast, start at 2:13:38, February 23, 2021, https://justthinking.me/ep-108-critical-race-theory/.

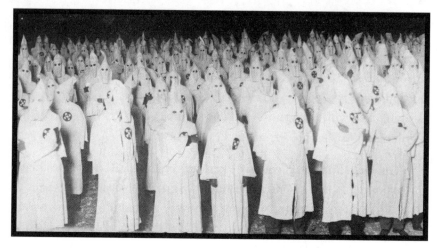

The Ku Klux Klan, infamous for their white robes and hoods, symbolizes a history of racial hatred and violence in America.

In a video of a training session that went viral, woke activist Ashleigh Shackelford articulated with shocking candor the status of white people in the CRT world.[15] To a room of mostly white people, she calmly told them that "all white people are racists." She went on to let them know they were hopeless to change, "No, you're always going to be racist, actually." But wait, there's more. In an amazing illustration of the caliber of ethnic hostility CRT creates, Shackelford continued, "I believe all white people are born into not being human." And then the mic drop, "And that's what y'all [white people] are taught to do, be demons." She said all that in the name of opposing racism! You might be thinking, "But that's about the most racist thing I've ever heard!" Well, silly rabbit, it's only racist if you define racism as racism. If you redefine racism to mean something other than racism, then racism isn't racist anymore. This is how CRT dodges such a problematic accusation and then weaponizes real racism in the name of justice as we'll see later. Her comments (though the last two are on the extreme end of the CRT spectrum or just not normally said out loud) accurately portray the plight of all whites in the CRT narrative. There is no hope, love, forgiveness, or reconciliation to be had. Only bitterness, blame, judgment, and unending penitence.

---

15 Grateful American, Ashleigh Shackelford - All White People are Racist, YouTube, September 9, 2020, https://www.youtube.com/watch?v=VAMofeTJpRk.

The more winsome CRT promoters try to soften this blow by telling whites you didn't choose this. It's just the system you were born into and shade of your skin that make you a dreadful oppressor. You're just born this way. Don't misunderstand, you're still condemned; but take solace in the fact that it's out of your control. As born oppressors, whites are destined to be part of a wicked, oppressive system that abuses, plunders, and enslaves people of color. Those involved in such atrocities cannot help but to have their consciences, even their souls, seared by the evil they're born into. Thus, some woke advocates like Ashleigh Shackelford radically conclude that whites are dehumanized and demonized. It is just their nature and lot as oppressive white people. Um, all of this is the literal definition of actual racism. It's a mountain of ethnic partiality.

How do blacks factor into the CRT racism equation? In short, blacks cannot be racist. You see, to be racist you must have systemic power says CRT. As we've seen, CRT is built on the premise that blacks do not have systemic power, so it is impossible for them to be racist. In an episode of Disney's rebooted cartoon *Proud Family* — an extremely woke show, the main character, Penny, a young black woman, is accused of being racist. She immediately responds, "Black people can't be racists!" And then another young black woman named Maya, the adopted daughter of a gay couple, profoundly states, "I agree, racism is prejudice plus power."[16] Bear in mind this show, full of critical theory ideology, is targeted toward kids. Those who have drunk from the CRT well want everyone to know that racism is only connected to whiteness — a sickness that plagues the white race alone. CRT imputes racism and guilt to whites, victimhood and innocence to blacks. Blacks are team angel; whites are team demon. Remember, CRT teaches there is only one sin: oppression. Thus, there is only one group of sinners: whites. Not only is it impossible for blacks to be racist, they can't even sin. The Bible has something to say about that.

Surely there is not a righteous man on earth who does good and never sins (Ecclesiastes 7:20).

---

16   Tony Turner, The Proud Family Says Black Ppl CAN'T Be Racist, YouTube, January 13, 2024, https://www.youtube.com/watch?v=jZf2_VQFBl4.

*If we say we have not sinned, we make him a liar, and his
word is not in us (1 John 1:10).*

For Christians who have syncretized with CRT doctrine, this directly
affects their understanding of the gospel. Since sin is systemic and not
individual, their new "gospel" isn't a call to die to self but for the death
of the current system. This is very much akin to Liberation Theology
in Latin America where salvation is essentially defined as liberating
the oppressed.[17] In CRT, the only "sinners" who need to repent are the
oppressors. The oppressed are innocent, powerless victims who have no
need of saving from judgment. In fact, since all oppressed minorities
are "sinless" by definition, any call for them to repent is manipulative
oppression; they have nothing to repent of. This is nothing less than the
death of the biblical gospel. Which is exclusive (no one's "in" by default of
their identity group), a need for every human soul, requires all to repent,
and shifts all power to Christ. All of which CRT fundamentally rejects
or redefines. The one true gospel of Jesus Christ that identifies all as
sinners and requires all to repent and believe for personal salvation is an
abomination to CRT.

And in CRT's dogma, the only moral standard for "good" is whatever
is done to overthrow the oppressive system and give power to the
oppressed. So, anything the oppressed blacks can do to overthrow the
tyranny of systemic racism in America is not only justified but praised as
virtuous. These are the "righteous acts" in CRT's "gospel" that culminate
in a culture's "salvation" as the oppressors are deposed and the oppressed
are empowered. This is an astounding license to sin and despise fellow
image bearers. While CRT arbitrarily defines goodness as shifting cultural
power, the Bible says that God alone is good and defines what is good.

*You are good and do good; teach me your statutes
(Psalm 119:68).*

---

17   Take for example this quote from Gustavo Gutierrez, regarded as one of the founders of Latin
     American Liberation Theology, "The theology of liberation is a theology of salvation in the con-
     crete, historical, and political conditions of our day." Source: Gustavo Gutierrez, *The Power of
     the Poor in History*: Selected Writings, translated by Robert Barr (Maryknoll: Orbis Books, 1983,
     originally published in Spanish by Centro de Estudios y Publicaciones, Lima, 1979), p. 63.

The Christopher Columbus statue outside the Minnesota State Capitol was toppled during racial justice protests after George Floyd's murder. Dakota and Ojibwe protesters saw Columbus as a symbol of genocide, colonialism, and dispossession.

Critical race theorists also dogmatically argue that any disparity in outcome between whites and blacks is racism manifest. You see this even in CRT's definitions for racism. It is assumed that racism "normalizes racial inequities," gives an "economic" advantage to the oppressors, affects the "outcomes of people's [oppressed blacks] lives." In any disparity of outcome, the question is always how did racism occur, not if. No other factors are allowed to be considered. No other conclusion is allowed to be entertained. The outcomes must be equal or it's racism.

If all that wasn't enough, if anyone disagrees with CRT, that's racism. Any white who disagrees is only trying to maintain oppressive power. Any black who disagrees is blind to their own oppression and is an unwitting ally for the oppressors. Every white or black who refuses to bow the knee to CRT's version of racism is exhibiting racism. Quite convenient and extremely fallacious. Carl Trueman, Christian professor and author of *The Rise and Triumph of the Modern Self*, makes this astute observation in an article on CRT,

> "Critical race theory, like other critical theories — postcolonialism or queer theory, for example — is self-certifying. Its basic claims, for example, that racism is systemic or that being non-racist is

impossible, are not conclusions drawn from arguments. They are axioms, and they cannot be challenged by those who do not agree with them. Those who dissent or offer criticism are, by definition, part of the problem."[18]

Sadly, once again, these anti-biblical ideas and definitions, in part or in whole, are taking residence in the minds and teachings of many professing Christians. We've already discussed how popular pastor Tim Keller indicted all whites of being "involved in injustice" and are "part of the problem" of racism. Barry Creamer, president of Criswell College — a Bible college — preached wholehearted CRT in an article for *The Dallas Morning News,*

> "I have spoken out in recent years encouraging Americans to acknowledge our corporate guilt in the ongoing racial injustice.... We have to address racism as a corporate problem.... In light of systemic racism's reality, what actions on my part are right?... For as long as America exists with its current institutions (may it be long) it will also need to be in group therapy where our turn begins with: 'Hi. I'm America, and I'm racist.'"[19]

Creamer's comments and perspective on racism would make any critical race theorist proud. Unfortunately, he is far from alone. Take, for example, David Platt, author of the bestselling book *Radical* and popular pastor of McLean Bible Church. In a sermon dealing with justice and racism at a T4G conference, Platt defined racism this way,

> "When I use that term [racism] I'm not just referring to the extremes that we often think of. Extremes that help us, particularly those of us who are white, distance ourselves from racism.... So here's the definition I'm using, a system ... in which race, and specifically as we're talking tonight black or white skin color, profoundly affects

18 Carl R. Trueman, "Evangelicals and Race Theory," *First Things,* February 2021, https://www.firstthings.com/article/2021/02/evangelicals-and-race-theory.

19 Barry Creamer, "Our faith and ethics must challenge our norms on race," *The Dallas Morning News,* August 9, 2020, https://www.dallasnews.com/opinion/commentary/2020/08/09/hi-im-america-and-im-racist/.

people's economic, political, and social experiences … a system of thought, practice that is ever subtly present among us, in me."[20]

Pastor Platt sounds like he's been taking notes from Kendi and DiAngelo. His definition of racism covers all the main CRT talking points. He starts off by letting us know that racism is not just about the extremists or "bad racists" as DiAngelo puts it. He implies that whites are apt to define racism only in terms of "bad racists" to avoid their culpability as mainstream racists. And notice his use of the term "system" in his definition of racism. Right in line with CRT ideology, Platt disconnects racism from its classic definition that focuses on the individual and shifts the meaning to a systemic oppression. This system, according to pastor Platt, affects outcomes of power and prosperity. Based on the rest of the sermon, and many other comments of his, the system relentlessly advantages whites. This system is "ever subtly present" because racism is systemic, and it is "in" Platt because he is white and is therefore part of the problem. These comments are not a "one off" for David Platt. In recent years he has made many statements that demonstrate he has jumped on the CRT bandwagon at some level. As with Matt Chandler and others, Platt appears to have an earnest desire for reconciliation which makes his comments all the more tragic. He's smuggling ideas into the church that only lead to division and hostility and undermine the very unity he seeks.

Let's examine just one more instance of CRT's infiltration into Christian thought on racism. For that we return to Matthew Hall, the former provost at SBTS and current provost and Senior Vice President at Biola University. In an online interview, he stared directly at the camera and said unflinchingly,

> "I am a racist…. I'm going to struggle with racism and white supremacy until the day I die and get my glorified body and a completely

---

20 Jono Brooks, 04 T4G 2018 David Platt Let Justice Roll Down Like Waters, Racism and our Need for Repentance, start at 22:37, YouTube, April 15, 2018, https://www.youtube.com/watch?v=9o9uHTmnzdY.

renewed and sanctified mind. Because I am immersed in a culture where I benefit from racism all the time."[21]

It's a safe bet when Hall says, "I am a racist," it doesn't mean he hates or maliciously hurts those with more melanin than him. His struggle with "racism and white supremacy" is in accordance with CRT definitions. He benefits from systemic racism automatically as a white person and is therefore automatically guilty and will continue to be until he gets to heaven. As Ashleigh Shackelford said, in this life there is no hope for whites of not being racist.

Friends, we are in the midst of a hostile takeover of our society and our vocabulary. For his own evil purposes, the enemy loves to take words and interpret them with his dictionary. CRT strategically seeks to redefine terms like racism, white supremacy, sin, good, justice, etc. to turn them into weapons for a Marxist revolution. To the detriment of the culture and church, many Christians and Christian leaders are using familiar words with new Marxist meanings. In such cases, their thoughts have been taken captive by an empty philosophy rooted in the traditions of man (Colossians 2:8). May we emulate the Bereans, testing all that we hear with the Scriptures (Acts 17:11), taking every thought captive for Christ, not Marx (2 Corinthians 10:5).

But if you have not yet fully embraced CRT with its new definitions and everything else it entails, it's time for you to get woke.

---

21 For the New Christian Intellectual, "I am a racist" — Matthew Hall, [former] Provost at Southern Seminary, YouTube, July 31, 2019, https://www.youtube.com/watch?v=1liKCYSevDU.

9

Get Woke or Get Canceled

Are you ready to get "woke?" I hope not. But what does this culturally popular word even mean? Comprehensively, to be woke means to be aware of, and attentive to, societal systemic oppressions that produce inequities and injustice, as defined by CRT. Early on, the term was primarily connected to racial injustice. As time progressed, it evolved to include a broader awareness of harm and oppression committed against women, the LGBTQ community, and even the climate. All of these are understood within the critical theory paradigm of oppressors and oppressed, and systemic racial injustice is still front and center. To be woke is to be awake to the world's true nature, as described by CRT, while the ignorant around you are sleepwalking.

To be woke: The Oppressed	To be woke: The Oppressors
The oppressed need to wake up to their systemic oppression and revolt, shifting cultural power to the oppressed by any means necessary.	The oppressors, "Whites," need to wake up to the reality of systemic oppression and their associated guilt. They must recognize their illicit gain as oppressors, give up their privilege, and work (without ceasing) to redistribute power, wealth, and influence to the oppressed to achieve equity.

Basically, everyone needs to wake up to CRT's projected reality of systemic oppression and respond the way critical race theorists tell us to. Becoming woke is akin to an awakening that reminds me of the movie *The Matrix*. In that movie, Neo, the main character, is offered the choice of two pills with very different consequences. If he takes the blue pill, he will stay plugged into the fantasy world, the Matrix, blissfully ignorant of the horrors of the real world. If he takes the red pill, he will be disconnected from the imaginary world and see the world how it truly is. Taking the red pill means giving up his illusory comfort, complacency, and current understanding of the world but it will be the truth. And once he knows the truth, he can then be about the business of battling the evils of reality, awakening others to their enslavement in a fantasy world and saving people from the vile system they're entrenched in whether they realize it or not. Wow, after saying all that it makes me wonder if the creators of the Matrix were critical theorists. This is what it means to be woke. CRT is the "red pill" that brings unsettling, life changing "truth" that calls for battle against the enslaving system and awakening others to the "truth."

As important as defining what woke is, equally important is clarifying what it is not. In his very helpful book *Christianity and Wokeness*, Owen Strachan has a whole section in chapter one clarifying "What Wokeness Is Not."[1] The section is so valuable I've borrowed the general concept, putting some of its points in my own words. I encourage you to check out his book for a deep dive into a practical understanding of wokeness and its impact on Christianity.

Wokeness Is Not:

≫ Recognizing the atrocities of racism, slavery, and discrimination in American and western history (1 Timothy 1:10, Exodus 21:16, Acts 10:34–35).

≫ Being profoundly disturbed by professing Christians' complicity with slavery and racism in the past (Deuteronomy 10:17, Galatians 2:11).

≫ Adopting children or marrying someone from a different ethnicity or with a different skin shade (Genesis 1:27, Acts 17:26, Galatians 3:28).

≫ Building relationships with people different from yourself and enjoying diverse cultures (Revelation 7:9-10).

---

1   Owen Strachan, *Christianity and Wokeness: How the Social Justice Movement Is Hijacking the Gospel — and the Way to Stop It,* (Washington, DC: Salem Books, 2021), p. 4–6.

≫ Grieving the tragic deaths of God's image bearers (Genesis 1:27, Psalm 139:15–16).

≫ Hating racism, the sin of partiality, and recognizing the potential for that sin in self or culture (2 Chronicles 19:7).

≫ Striving for greater justice in a broken world and caring for those in need (Micah 6:8, Isaiah 58:6–8).

≫ Wanting societal reconciliation and harmony across different backgrounds, ethnicities, and skin shades (Romans 12:17–18, Colossians 3:13, Hebrews 12:14).

All of these things, rightly understood, come straight from the biblical worldview. Actually, the Bible alone provides the only foundation to rightly define these principles and actions as good and right. Again, without the absolute authority of God and His revealed Word, why would slavery, partiality, murder, injustice, hypocrisy, or hate be wrong? Having a deep concern for fellow image bearers of God and a hatred for sin is profoundly biblical and God honoring. One really must ask why the secularists, with no God or absolute morality, care about any of these things. They care because they are made in God's image and know intuitively that some things are right, and some are wrong. Now that intuition has been marred by sin, and so we see the misapplication of their God-given conscience. But from their heart of hearts, God's truth speaks forth.

Within CRT thinking, it seems generally assumed that the oppressed in modern society are going to be woke or are rapidly on their way. It is presumed they will likely be "red pilled" by any number of factors and in agreement with wokeness.[2] But what if someone from an oppressed group isn't woke, refuses to get woke, or even fights against wokeness? Does that mean the woke ideology of CRT is wrong? Nope. They're just still "asleep."

---

2   It seems critical theorists vary on the means of the awakening of the oppressed. Some lean towards the idea of oppression itself being the "red pill." This is more classically Marxist but conflicts with Gramsci's idea of hegemony. For others, presumably a multitude of current societal forces and voices lead to the awakening. There may also be those who combine these ideas or point to something else. Either way, CRT generally assumes the oppressed will be woke or are well on their way.

Lulled into a deep slumber by the lies of systemic racism, they've normalized their oppression and thus stay comfortably plugged into the "Matrix." Someone or something just needs to wake them up. Yet again, no matter what, CRT and wokeism must be true. It's unfalsifiable. It's an all-inclusive worldview, without a consistent foundation, which demands everything be explained within its own paradigm to its own affirmation.

That being said, the fervent focus of woke evangelists is to "red pill" the oppressors who are the primary cause of society's injustices and inequities. To lift the veil of their blindness that they may see the egregious sin of systemic oppression for which the oppressors alone are responsible — calling them to acknowledge their inherited and innate guilt, along with their accumulated guilt in supporting, contributing, expanding, and benefitting from the oppression. Those in the oppressor group do this by simply existing. Urging them to repent of the unjust privileges and rewards they've enjoyed life-long at the dire expense of others. And commissioning them to follow the commandments of wokeism to redistribute power and resources to the oppressed. This is to be done for an "atonement" the oppressor can never fully accomplish and to achieve the Neo-Marxist utopia of societal equity. All of this comes with a warning as well, either voluntarily bow the knee to the god of wokeness or face judgment. For those who refuse wokeness, they face

The Calgary Women's March to promote the feminist agenda.

the wrath of public shaming, coercion, cultural banishment, and forced obscurity. Woke ideologues only put two options on the table, either get woke or get canceled. Gotta love the zealous, unyielding intolerance of the self-professed tolerant.

As we've already seen in previous chapters, many Christians are introducing wokeness into the church and other Christian institutions. Matthew Hall[3] from Biola, who's been quoted a couple of times now, was congratulated on an interview with the woke Jude 3 Project, "You are what we call, becoming more awake."[4] In other words, woke. Tragically, so many other Christians, some with huge platforms, could receive the same woke commendation. I do not know the motivations of those compromising with woke ideas. But one must wonder if the desire for a woke "pat on the back," or a fear of being "canceled," is at least part of the equation.

As stated earlier, to be woke today typically involves embracing any number of secular causes rooted in critical theory rationale. Things like heteronormativity (biblical sexuality), the gender binary (only two genders), scriptural masculinity/femininity, marriage, the family, are all considered part of the system of oppression. These things, with their biblical undergirding, are all understood to be oppressive societal structures founded by the oppressors to establish and enshrine their power. They're all part of a scheme that is meant to dominate the oppressed and unendingly benefit the oppressors. In response, abortion (preborn baby murder) is meant to liberate women. Destroying the nuclear family is meant to abolish the institution that transmits, from one generation to another, the principles that preserve oppression. Redefining gender, sexuality, and marriage is meant to liberate "sexual minorities"— those operating outside of biblical sexuality. And so, it goes on. Woke culture views Christianity itself as an

---

3   It is worth noting that Matthew Hall, since making the comments quoted in this book, has gone on public record to denounce CRT. Link to his statement below. This is good news and brings up other questions articulated well in the second link. https://equip.sbts.edu/article/peace-centrality-gospel-christ-racial-reconciliation/. https://founders.org/articles/matthew-halls-rejection-of-critical-race-theory/.

4   KineticsLive, Confronting Racist Evangelical History- Dr. Otis Moss III and Dr. Matthew Hall, YouTube, May 12, 2016, start at 23:40, https://www.youtube.com/watch?v=Qx-7LrvJmsk.

engine of oppression. That's why it vehemently attacks God's created order and design, established in Genesis 1–11.

Once you understand this, you can see why standing on the authority of God's Word from the very first verse is absolutely vital. The real history of Genesis 1–11 is necessary to address both the scientific questions and the social issues of this age. When the devil said to Eve in Genesis 3, "Did God really say?" he was attacking the authority of God's Word. Likewise, the enemy has used the lies of evolution and millions of years to undercut people's trust in God's Word from the beginning. He's been attacking biblical history, to undermine biblical authority, to undermine the biblical doctrines and gospel rooted in that authority. Because if you can't trust what the Bible clearly says at the beginning, why trust the middle or the end? Not only that, the history of Genesis 1–11 is the foundation for the Christian worldview, all biblical doctrines (directly or indirectly), and the gospel itself.

You see, the lies of evolution and millions of years aren't just used by the devil to undermine creation and biblical authority. He's also attacking the foundation for every single biblical doctrine, including the doctrines we need to refute the woke ideologies of our age. How do we know marriage is between one man and one woman for life? How do we know there are only two genders? How do we know the proper boundaries of sex and sexuality? How do we know there is only one race? How do we know every human being has equal, inherent value because they are made in God's image? How do we explain the brokenness of this world? How do we justify the need for the Last Adam without the real history of the first Adam? It all goes back to the true history of Genesis 1–11. The answers to origins and society's problems are found in Genesis.

Make no mistake, the woke ideology is an attack on God's created order and design, biblical authority, and the gospel. What Genesis calls good, wokeness calls evil (Isaiah 5:20). So many today are being seduced by a woke melody. Leading younger generations away from "bigoted, intolerant, oppressive" Christianity in droves and causing a tsunami of compromise within the church. What can Christians do? How can we be

LGBTQ+ flags being flown at a pride parade.

woke-proof? Trust and apply God's Word, all of it — starting in Genesis 1. Equipping ourselves and the coming generations with a biblical world-view and the answers it provides to unmask woke ideas for the oppressive evil they are.

To be woke is to fall for the lies of the enemy. The sad irony is wokeness makes a person blind and unaware, asleep to the true nature of the world as rightly defined by its Creator. The deceptions and fabrications of the enemy and this present age are the actual "Matrix." The true reality that every person needs to wake up to is the fact that God is God; we're not. His Word is the authority; ours is not. We all have sinned, deserve God's wrath, and desperately need a Savior. When Jesus appeared to Paul on the road to Damascus, He said He was sending him as a witness to the gentiles,

> *"... to open their eyes, so that they may turn from darkness to light and from the power of Satan to God, that they may receive forgiveness of sins and a place among those who are sanctified by faith in me" (Acts 26:18).*

This is the real "red pill" every human needs, no matter their skin shade. But once you're woke, you're ready to listen to, and obey, oppressed voices.

The Authority
of Oppressed Voices

10

Critical race theorists view the oppressed as inevitably "red pilled." Those who have endured the experience of systemic racism have been awakened to societal realities that others are blind to, by ignorance or choice. The oppressed see the "Matrix" (societal structure) for what it is: an engineered enslaving system created explicitly to benefit the oppressors. The secret knowledge of the awakened oppressed is the key to liberating society if others will listen. In the American context, blacks, as the primary oppressed group, are the awakened ones. Their lived experience has opened their eyes and given them a deeper knowledge of society that whites, as oppressors, simply can't have. Tara Yosso, professor and often cited CRT authority, says it like this,

> "CRT recognizes that the **experiential knowledge of People of Color** is legitimate, appropriate, and **critical to understanding**, analyzing, and teaching about *racial subordination*"[1] (emphasis and italics added).

In the book *Words that Wound*, an all-star list of critical race theorists echoes this same sentiment as a "defining element" of CRT,

> "Critical race theory *insists* on recognition of the **experiential knowledge of people of color**.... This knowledge is gained from critical reflection on the **lived experience of racism**"[2] (emphasis and italics added).

1 Tara J. Yosso, *Whose Culture Has Capital? A Critical Race Theory Discussion of Community Cultural Wealth, Race Ethnicity and Education* 8, no.1, March 2005, p. 74, https://www.tandfonline.com/doi/abs/10.1080/1361332052000341006.
2 Mari J Matsuda, Charles R. Lawrence III, Richard Delgado, Kimberle Williams Crenshaw, *Words That Wound: Critical Race Theory, Assaultive Speech, And The First Amendment* (New York, NY: Routledge, 2018), p. 6.

As mentioned in a previous chapter, CRT ideology believes that knowledge is a social construct, and that objective truth is a myth imposed by whiteness. CRT asserts that all knowledge produced in a society reflects the ideals and desires of its makers. All means of knowing are filtered through a biased cultural setting. Different cultural contexts provide different experiences, which lead to different realms and ways of knowing. Thus, truth and knowledge are subjectively determined by lived experience. For oppressors to say there's one universal truth for all is to tyrannically impose their truth on a culture and dismiss marginalized lives and voices. This is how CRT equates objective truth to white supremacy, white privilege, and systemic racism. To claim absolute truth is to assert "white truth" and that whiteness is rightness.

Of course you know, if someone says there are no absolutes, the first question you need to ask is, "Is that absolutely true?" The statement itself is inherently inconsistent. It blows itself up by its own standard. I can't help but point out once more that no absolute truth means all morality is relative and opinion based. If that's the case, there's no absolute reason to say anything, including oppression, is immoral. Nothing is unfair or unjust; it's all just molecules in motion with survival of the fittest or luckiest. So, what are CRT advocates complaining about? But all of that is just logic, which is also deemed by CRT as part of the edifice of whiteness

Rally participants entering Emancipation Park in Charlottesville, Virginia, on August 12, 2017, carrying Neo-Confederate, Confederate battle, Gadsden, Nazi, and other flags.

and systemic oppression. It's interesting how critical race theorists will use logic to make their case and then demonize it whenever it suits them.

Regardless of logic or consistency, CRT says truth is defined by experience and whatever brings revolutionary social change. All that shifts cultural power from the oppressor to the oppressed is good and true. Blacks, as the oppressed and enlightened, are uniquely equipped by their experience to lead the blind — the whites — into truth. And let's be clear, whites are entirely blinded by CRT estimation, plugged into the "Matrix" of whiteness. Eric Mason, pastor of Epiphany Fellowship and author of *Woke Church*, emphatically communicates this CRT tenet in a sermon with escalating passion and volume,

> "The noetic effects of sin is the negative effects of sin on the minds and thinking of humankind, causing the reasoning ability of fallen humanity to be corrupted.... Ephesians 4:18 … says, 'having their understanding darkened … because. Of. The. Blindness. Of. Their. Heart.' **Whiteness. Has. Caused. Blind. Ness. Of. Heart. Whiteness. Has. Caused. Blind. Ness. Of. HEART!**"[3] (emphasis added).

Pastor Mason does hermeneutical gymnastics to twist Ephesians 4:18 into saying whiteness, which is intrinsic only to whites, darkens understanding. Whiteness causes blindness. By CRT calculation, not only are whites racist, white supremacist, oppressive, and guilty because of their skin shade; they're also born blind and ignorant. Helpless to see or change or make penitence unless enlightened black voices open their eyes to see their innate desperate and destitute oppressive state. I do not use this language to be inflammatory. I use it to convey, in the clearest possible terms, the reality of CRT's racist and divisive impulses. To declare a whole group of people inherently ignorant based on their skin alone is the textbook definition of racism. The sin of ethnic partiality is the lifeblood of CRT.

---

3   Woke Preacher Clips, Eric Mason: *"Whiteness Has Caused Blindness of Heart!"* YouTube, September 23, 2020, https://www.youtube.com/watch?v=O-O6Ufo3GH8.

Phil Vischer, creator of Veggie Tales®, has also turned to the woke-side. In recent years, he has made a litany of statements that flow right out of the CRT worldview. In this tweet, he too conveys the need for whites to listen to oppressed voices as authoritative,

> "The Bible can't tell us what it's like to be black in America, or how to address systemic discrimination in housing or education…. We need to **listen to voices** who study the issues and have had the **experience.**"[4]

Again, only the voices of those who have the lived experience of enduring systemic racism are deemed culturally credible. In the same thread Vischer says,

> "I don't think we're [whites] the ones who get to decide who 'gets it' when it comes to race in America. `Kay?"[5]

Oppressive whites do not get to speak to the racism they've systemically instituted and maintained. Their only role is to listen to, learn from, and unquestionably follow awakened black voices. Dr. Voddie Baucham summarizes well the situation according to CRT,

> "If black people know racism, and white people cannot know racism (and are racist by default as a result of their white privilege), then the only acceptable response is for white people to sit down, shut up, and listen to what black people have to say on the matter."[6]

But that's not all. CRT insists that whites cannot challenge the experiential knowledge and exalted voices of oppressed blacks. If they do, I bet you guessed it, that's racist. Any push back at all is just whites trying to maintain their power and white privilege. So, whites can either agree they're racist and quietly listen, or verbalize any disagreement at all and

---

4   Phil Vischer (@philvischer), Twitter, June 9, 2020, https://twitter.com/philvischer/status/1270468029093216257.

5   Ibid.

6   Voddie Baucham, Fault Lines: The Social Justice Movement and Evangelicalism's Looming Catastrophe (New York, NY: Salem Books, 2021), p. 103.

Protesting school censorship in the United States.

that just proves they're racist. It's a win, win for CRT and a lose, lose for logic and societal unity.

Not only must all whites agree with CRT, but also all blacks. Since all blacks are systemically oppressed, it must be that all blacks are awakened and therefore will have the same CRT affirming perspective. If a black person does not uphold the CRT narrative that doesn't mean CRT is wrong. It just means that particular black is broken and has "internalized" their oppression. CRT argues that if an oppressed black rejects the notion of their oppression, that just shows how thorough and insidious the oppression is. They've been deceived by their own oppression into believing the systemic oppression they live with is normal and even good for them. This notion, called "false consciousness,"[7] is concisely articulated by Carl Trueman,

> "Critical theory ... relies on the concept of false consciousness — the notion that the oppressors control society so completely that the oppressed believe their own interests are served by the status quo. This is a wonderful idea. It allows every piece of evidence that might

---

7   Some critical theorists, like Herbert Marcuse, relate "false consciousness" more directly to hegemony, effectively blinding all, oppressor and oppressed alike, within an oppressive society. The end result is still the same.

refute one's theory to be transformed into further evidence of how deep and comprehensive the problem of oppression is."[8]

Everything is racist, everything proves oppression, every time CRT is unfalsifiable because it is a conspiratorial worldview. Nonetheless, blacks who refuse CRT's victim ideology, or dare to fight against it, are extremely problematic for critical race theorists. They can be used as pawns by the oppressors to dismiss claims of oppression, repress revolution, and continue masquerading oppression as society. Not only are these "un-woke" blacks part of the problem, they're also widely considered traitors. They're enabling a system that abuses and enslaves their own people. As a result, blacks who refuse the CRT indoctrination are often deemed by blacks who embrace it, as pseudo-blacks. They may look black on the outside but they're not really black through and through. They're derisively called names like "sell-out negroes," "Uncle Toms," "skinfolk but not kinfolk," or "Oreos"— black on the outside and white on the inside. Take for example the time when Larry Elder, a conservative black political commentator, ran for governor in California in 2021. The *Los Angeles Times* ran a column by Erika Smith, a black woman, entitled "Larry Elder is the Black face of white supremacy. You've been warned." Elder is seen

Black Lives Matter symbol.

8   Carl R. Trueman, *Evangelicals and Race Theory*, *First Things*, February 2021, https://www. firstthings.com/article/2021/02/evangelicals-and-race-theory.

as a big problem because he "is someone who just fundamentally doesn't believe that [systemic racism] exists." Here are a couple of quotes from the article which is dripping with CRT and animosity for a non-woke black,

> "Like a lot of Black people, though, I've learned that it's often best just to ignore people like Elder. People who are — as my dad used to say — 'skinfolk' but not necessarily kinfolk."

> "'He is a danger, a clear and present danger,' said Melina Abdullah, co-founder of Black Lives Matter Los Angeles."

> "Anytime you put a black face on white supremacy, which is what Larry Elder is, there are people who will utilize that as an opportunity to deny white supremacy…. But everything that he's pushing, everything that he stands for, he is advancing white supremacy."[9]

It's hard to put into words how bigoted and prejudice CRT ideology is. If you're white, you're racist, if you're black you're awakened and enlightened, unless you're not, in which case you're not really black. Darrell Harrison hit the nail on the head when he said,

> "CRT is a multi-layer cake, with each layer having a different color, but it's frosted in the end with the same flavor of racist icing from top to bottom."[10]

All in all, the racist ideology of CRT makes the lived experiences and inner feelings of *agreeing* blacks the authority and arbiter for truth. This is brazenly anti-biblical and must be rejected by Christians. God alone defines truth because He is truth, and His Word is truth (Psalm 18:30, John 14:6, 17:17, Hebrews 6:18). We are to follow Christ not feelings. The Bible makes it crystal clear that no one, no matter their skin shade, should

---

9   Erika D. Smith, "Larry Elder is the Black Face of White Supremacy. You've Been Warned," *Los Angeles Times*, August 20, 2021, https://www.latimes.com/california/story/2021-08-20/recall-candidate-larry-elder-is-a-threat-to-black-californians.

10 Darrell B. Harrison, "Episode 108 Critical Race Theory," *Just Thinking* Podcast, start at 1:41:37, February 23, 2021, https://justthinking.me/ep-108-critical-race-theory/.

embrace Disney's mantra of "follow your heart." God's Word tells us in Jeremiah 17:9,

> *The heart is deceitful above all things, and desperately sick;*
> *who can understand it?*

Following our heart/feelings, looking inward for truth, is a terrible idea because our feelings are pulled toward depravity by the immense gravity of our sin nature. A society that equates feelings with goodness is asking for chaos and is likely, if not determined, to "call evil good and good evil" (Isaiah 5:20).

When it comes to listening to the voices in our culture, Christians should be "quick to hear, slow to speak, slow to anger" (James 1:19). Willing to "Rejoice with those who rejoice, weep with those who weep" (Romans 12:15). Compassionately and sincerely engaging people in an effort to learn, understand, and to love. But, as we do, we must be like the Bereans who faithfully went about "examining the Scriptures daily to see if these things were so" (Acts 17:11). We take *everything* back to the word of God. It is the authority over feelings, experiences, perceptions of reality, everything. God's Word is the authority, *not* man's experience!

But if you argue against any of this as a white person, that's just your "white fragility" showing.

11

White Fragility

White fragility — if you're white, you've got it. You might be saying to yourself, "But I don't want it." CRT says too bad, it just comes with being white in this cultural context. So, what exactly is this dreadful sounding syndrome that plagues whites and where did it come from? Dictionary. com defines white fragility this way,

> "the tendency among members of the dominant white cultural group to have a defensive, wounded, angry, or dismissive response to evidence of racism."[1]

But it is so much more than that. It originates from the caldron of CRT thinking, specifically from renowned CRT evangelist Robin DiAngelo. She is a professor, consultant, and author with focused research in Whiteness Studies and Critical Discourse Analysis. Based on this alone you can tell where she is coming from. In 2011, DiAngelo coined the term "White Fragility" in an academic article. In 2018, her book *White Fragility: Why It's So Hard for White People to Talk about Racism* was released. It is a *New York Times* bestseller, remained on the bestseller list for over three years, and it's been translated into 12 languages. The immense popularity of her work has opened many doors — in media, universities, corporations, government agencies[2] — for the transmission of her CRT saturated ideas. Since white fragility is DiAngelo's idea, I'll let her tell you what it is in more detail. Before I do, I believe it is important to note, for the context of the quotes, that Robin DiAngelo is a white woman. She freely admits that she struggles with white fragility, just like all other white people, and includes herself in the quotes. That being said, let's go through a series of

---

1   https://www.dictionary.com/browse/white-fragility.

2   Daniel Bergner, "'White Fragility' Is Everywhere. But Does Antiracism Training Work?" *The New York Times Magazine,* July 15, 2020, https://www.nytimes.com/2020/07/15/magazine/white-fragility-robin-diangelo.html.

quotes from a video that DiAngelo made with *The Guardian* that concisely summarize white fragility.

> "White fragility is the defensiveness, the argumentation, the hurt feelings, the withdrawal, that often erupts whenever white people are challenged on their racial worldviews."[3]

As with whiteness, white fragility is an issue that belongs to the white oppressors alone. Because no one else can be defensive, argumentative, or erupt when they are challenged on their racial worldviews, right? Once again, CRT says that only the oppressors, and all the oppressors, are the problem. Whites are automatically guilty, and the oppressed blacks can't be because of their lack of cultural power. If blacks are confrontational or explode toward whites, that is seen as just and good because they're working to redistribute societal power to the oppressed. DiAngelo continues,

> "The fragility part is meant to capture how little it takes to cause white people to erupt in defensiveness."[4]

3   Guardian News, "How 'White Fragility' Reinforces Racism," YouTube, June 26, 2020, https://www.youtube.com/watch?v=YvIO2GU8yTU.

4   Ibid.

If you think back to the chapter on whiteness, there were whole lists of negative attributes intrinsically assigned to whites by CRT believers. Whites, as an identity group, were basically called arrogant, defensive, ignorant, and dismissive; this is the sort of fragility DiAngelo is referring to. It would seem whites are painted as an unenlightened bully who has unfair power but is actually insecure, that's why he so quickly pummels anyone who challenges him. What also appears to be implied here is that whites know in their heart of hearts they're guilty of oppression. That's why it takes so little for them to "erupt in defensiveness." Like the child who gets caught doing wrong but then throws a fit, dramatically proclaiming their innocence and blaming others, hoping that their emotional display will con their parents. It is their knowledge of guilt that causes such a dramatic and adverse reaction. And just as the child throws the tantrum in an attempt to get their way, so do whites,

> "But the impact of that defensiveness however is not fragile at all. It functions as a kind of everyday white racial control by making it so difficult for people to challenge us on our unaware assumptions and biases that most of the time they don't. And so it functions to keep everybody in their place and protect the racial hierarchy."[5]

We all know that person — a family member, friend, co-worker, etc. — who we avoid criticizing at all costs because we know we will feel their wrath. Or we will be annoyed to death by their compulsive desire to passionately defend and justify themselves. Just one negative sentiment directed their way and it's on. It's just easier, and much more peaceful, to leave them be, even if they're in the wrong. Their anger is a weapon they yield to maintain power and control. So it is with whites according to critical race theory. In her book, DiAngelo describes it this way,

> "Though white fragility is triggered by discomfort and anxiety, it is born of superiority and entitlement. White fragility is not weakness

---

5   Ibid.

per se. In fact, it is a powerful means of white racial control and the protection of white advantage."[6]

First, note that the entitlement DiAngelo is referring to comes straight from the fabricated superiority that whites supposedly created known as whiteness. The white fragility of whites, their over-the-top defensiveness, is meant to be a means of "white racial control" to ensure white comfort and privilege, suppressing blacks in order to maintain the "racial hierarchy" with whites on top. It's a power play to keep anyone from challenging the hegemony, the biased structure of society, established by whites for their benefit. As DiAngelo states further in the video, "racism is the status quo" and creates a society that is comfortable and advantageous for white people.

So what counts as excessive defensiveness? What amount of negative reaction or argumentation rises to the level of white fragility? Any amount. It's the same thing we've already seen a couple of times now. Whites only have two options, both of which establish them as privileged racists and white supremacists. They can either accept their guilt, and work to fight against systemic racism as DiAngelo has, or they can deny their guilt, for any reason and in any way, and that's their white fragility showing, which proves they're racist. The analytical lens of CRT will allow no other outcome. But as already discussed, this is a "catch 22" and logically fallacious. Assuming your conclusion by smuggling it into the argument does not prove your conclusion. To use a classic example, it's like asking someone the question, "Have you stopped beating your wife?" What's he going to say? If he says yes, that means he used to beat his wife. If he says no, that means he's still beating his wife. Either way, by this argumentation, he is guilty of beating his wife. The original question snuck in the assumption of the person's guilt before they could even answer. If the question is not allowed to be examined or reframed then the guilt of the accused is assured. Likewise, CRT advocates have created an argument they can't

6   Robin J. DiAngelo, *White Fragility: Why It's So Hard for White People to Talk about Racism* (Boston, MA: Beacon Press, 2018), p. 2.

lose. I appreciate the way Darrell Harrison describes this. He says CRT activists have "hit the dialectical lottery" because they,

> "have the luxury ... of making self-certifying, broad-based general-izations, assertions, and accusations of systemic oppression without fear of having those generalizations, assertions, and accusations challenged, at the risk of [the opposer] being labeled a racist or white supremacist."[7]

He continues by saying that the CRT pundit can then go on to demand essentially any reparation without concern of refusal for the same reason. This should remind us once again, that critical race theorists are not trying to prove systemic oppression. Their worldview assumes it and demands that you assume it as well. Ultimately, the language of the critical theorist is manipulative, deceptive, slanderous, and consequently perverse. The Word of God instructs us,

> *Put away from you crooked speech, and put devious talk*
> *far from you (Proverbs 4:24).*

> *Better is a poor person who walks in his integrity than one*
> *who is crooked in speech and is a fool (Proverbs 19:1).*

---

7   Darrell Harrison, Episode 108 Critical Race Theory, *Just Thinking* Podcast, start at 1:53:52, February 23, 2021, https://justthinking.me/ep-108-critical-race-theory/.

And oh, the hypocrisy.[8] DiAngelo goes on to lament the dismissive close-mindedness of whites and white fragility,

> "it's defensiveness that functions to refuse to engage. To protect a very limited worldview, to let in no information and no challenge."[9]

But CRT is literally a "very limited worldview" that does not allow contradicting information or any challenge to its validity. In her absolute worldview of no absolutes, DiAngelo is saying it is absolutely wrong to assume your worldview is absolute. It's not wrong for critical race theorists to absolutely assume the reality and rightness of their worldview, but it is wrong for anyone else. It is again evident that the CRT worldview is fundamentally hypocritical and radically inconsistent. It can't help but be so because it was born in the minds of men.

Let's sum up. Along with being racist oppressors, whites, by virtue of being white, are deemed childish, abusive bullies who throw fits to manipulate and maintain illegitimate power. They're just born that way. And it's not racist to assumptively believe that because the oppressed, and anything that reallocates societal power to the oppressed, can't be racist. If you're white and disagree, that's just your white fragility manifesting itself. If you're black and disagree, you're still plugged into the "Matrix" and are currently the black face of white supremacy. Critical race theorists boldly assume and assert all these things and confidently say "just trust us and do what we say." But as we've seen, God's Word is vigorously opposed to the fundamental pillars of CRT on almost every imaginable front. And God says,

> *Trust in the Lord with all your heart, and do not lean on*
> *your own understanding (Proverbs 3:5).*

---

8   Some may try to dismiss this by saying Christians are hypocrites too. Which is true. Really, in a sense, any time a Christian sins they're being hypocritical, and we won't be perfect until we're with Christ. Thus, Christians are called to confess their sin, and to strive to consistently follow Christ. But only the Christian worldview, with absolute truth and morality, can consistently say hypocrisy is wrong. If there are no absolutes, hypocrisy can't be bad and is not even possible. And because all humans are made in God's image, we intuitively know hypocrisy is wrong.

9   *Guardian News*, "How 'white fragility' reinforces racism," YouTube, June 26, 2020, https://www.youtube.com/watch?v=YvIO2GU8yTU.

As established at the beginning of this book, either God's Word or man's word is your authority. There is no neutrality, and no one can serve two masters. Everyone has faith and must choose where they will put it.

But once you're woke and have gotten over all your white fragility, it's time to get to the unending work of anti-racism.

12

Anti-racism

Sounds so good, right? I mean who doesn't want to be known for being anti-racist? What's the alternative, pro-racism? Especially Christians who understand the intrinsic dignity and value possessed by every individual made in God's image. With today's cultural climate and the exceptionally positive moral connotations of putting "anti" with "racism," this CRT buzzword has recently exploded onto the American scene. Books, media, classes, training for corporate and federal employees, it's everywhere. But as is often the case with CRT ideas and language, things are not what they appear to be. Here is what critical race theorists mean by anti-racism:

Anti-racism: 1. *Actively* fighting racism as *defined* by **CRT**. **2.** Working to **dismantle** and replace the **systemically racist** structures of society to achieve **equity.**

It must be understood that when CRT activists talk about being anti-racist and fighting racism, they're referring to their definition of racism. Glancing back at chapter 8 you'll recall that CRT defines racism as, "systemic, institutional, and corporate bias that advantages one group." The CRT understanding of racism focuses primarily on "systems," as Pastor Platt put it, not individuals. In fact, CRT declares you can have racism without individual racists because it's embedded into society.

When most people first hear the term "anti-racism," they're thinking of fighting racism by its "old," actual definition. Defending the equality of all people — combatting beliefs, attitudes, words, and actions that demean, devalue, and attack other human beings based solely on physical traits. This is not what CRT means by anti-racism. For critical race theorists, anti-racism is all about tearing down society's assumed systemically oppressive structures, in order to rebuild and ultimately create a

Neo-Marxist utopia. And since CRT decisively proclaims that everything in American culture is racist, the whole thing needs to be replaced. I'll say it again — critical race theorists want to tear down American society so that it can be built back Marxist.

And if you don't want to be racist, this is something you must do. You must be actively fighting racism, as CRT defines it, or you are a racist. There is no middle ground. Ibram X. Kendi, an anti-racist scholar and CRT superstar, makes this clear. Kendi is a professor at Boston University, prolific author, and is widely esteemed as the ultimate anti-racism guru. His book *How to Be an Antiracist,* a #1 *New York Times* bestseller, is the premier textbook of schools, organizations, corporations, and government agencies on how to fight racism. In it he says this,

> "What's the problem with being 'not racist'? It is a claim that signifies neutrality: 'I am not a racist, but neither am I aggressively against racism.' But there is no neutrality in the racism struggle. **The opposite of 'racist' isn't 'not racist.' It is 'anti-racist'**"[1] (emphasis added).

Neutrality is not an option. Either you're aggressively struggling against CRT's version of racism or you're a racist. And passivity is still racist. Maybe you've seen the slogan "white silence is violence." Refusing to

---

1   Ibram X. Kendi, *How to Be an Antiracist* (New York, NY: One World, 2019), p. 9.

speak out and get involved is considered an active choice that helps perpetuate systemic racism. Basically, you either agree with CRT and respond accordingly or you are the problem. Of course, white people are already deemed innately racist because of their identity as oppressors. But choosing not to fight, as prescribed by CRT, means you're not just a racist by birth, you're a racist by choice. The worst of the worst.

This too has entered the realm of Christian thought. Jemar Tisby, author of *Color of Compromise* and leading evangelical woke voice, concisely shared this same sentiment in an interview with Phil Vischer.

> "Black people ... have not been given our due in terms of equity ... distribution of resources ... opportunity and it speaks to the idea that we have to be intentional and be actively working to ensure equity and justice ... you are either actively working against racism, or you are supporting racism, whether actively or passively; there's no in-between."[2]

In the rest of the clip, Tisby throws in some Bible references and "Christianese" but it's the same CRT talking points.

What is the goal of the work of anti-racism? Tisby mentions that in the clip as well — "to ensure equity and justice" — equity and justice within the parameters of CRT. In CRT thinking, justice is equity, and equity demands that everyone receives the same outcome, full stop. Any disparity in outcomes between oppressed blacks and oppressor whites is purely the result of systemic racism.[3] And since whites rigged society's rules to always advantage whites, whites have illegitimately amassed wealth, power, and privilege to the oppressive detriment of blacks. What could have been acquired by blacks in a fair society has been stolen by systemic

2 Woke Preacher Clips, Jemar Tisby Defines What He Means By "Racial Justice" And "Equity," YouTube, February 2, 2021, https://www.youtube.com/watch?v=saDG8Aw7kUA.

3 Critics may respond that some studies do show disparate outcomes between different ethnic neighborhoods, in healthcare access, etc. Two quick thoughts. One, there can be multiple complex causes for disparities, including family breakdown/fatherlessness, which Voddie Baucham discusses in detail in *Faultlines* (p. 153–176). Two, if in certain cases partiality is indeed the culprit, God's Word alone consistently gives us the foundation to identity that as a problem and rightly address it.

racism and white privilege. In the quest for just equity, a primary part of the work of anti-racism is to redistribute wealth, power, privilege, and opportunities to the oppressed.

Enter DEI, Diversity-Equity-Inclusion. The whole premise of DEI is that **diverse** groups must be **included** in societal opportunities to achieve justice and **equity.** On the face of it, this is right and good. But here's the problem, the focus on including the "diverse" usually comes with the dismissal of the "non-diverse." Who are the "diverse"? The oppressed, primarily blacks but also all other minorities. Basically, anyone other than whites. The "non-diverse" are those oppressive whites who have benefited far too long from an unjust system. More times than not, DEI is CRT philosophy manifest. Seeking to redistribute societal goods, power, and opportunities from the oppressors to the oppressed in the name of equity.

What this means practically is that opportunities for jobs, scholarships, positions of power and influence, and so on, are offered primarily to the oppressed. So, you can get a job or not get a job, get a scholarship or not get a scholarship, based solely on the shade of your skin. There's a word for that: racism. Or discrimination if you prefer. Either way, it is biblically understood as sinful partiality. Not only that, but the typical DEI training imposed on employees and students in the name of creating a safe environment is usually straight CRT, like what we saw with Coca-Cola® and Walmart earlier. And you don't have to be Sherlock Holmes to find DEI and anti-racism at work in our culture today. They are repeatedly showing up in various ways in America's current heightened CRT climate. Here are just a few examples:

➤ **"Arizona State University professor sues school over DEI training: 'simply racism'"[4]**
"The training, titled 'ASU Inclusive Communities,' teaches faculty and staff that "white supremacy [is] normalized in society…." The course

---

4   Kendal Tietz, "Arizona State University professor sues school over DEI training: 'simply racism," Fox News, March 20, 2024, https://www.foxnews.com/media/arizona-state-universi-ty-professor-sues-school-dei-training-simply-racism.

also discusses how to "critique whiteness" and other topics like "white privilege"; "white fragility"; and the need for "transformative justice."

≫ **"Chicago's Art Institute Fires All of Its Docents: Too Many Wealthy White Ladies"[5]**
Getting rid of the oppressors to open opportunities for the oppressed. This is doing the woke work of anti-racism.

≫ **"San Francisco Company Twilio Announces 'Anti-Racist' Layoff Policy"[6]**
The CEO proudly stated, "We were particularly focused on ensuring our layoffs — while a business necessity today — were carried out through an anti-racist/anti-oppression lens." Translation: we just fired a lot of people for being white.

≫ **"The Votes of Black Americans Should Count Twice"[7]**
Brandon Hasbrouck, assistant professor at Washington and Lee University School of Law, is the author of the article. In it he says, "Because white votes currently count more than Black ones, double-counting Black votes would restore electoral balance…. To address systemic racism, we must transform how we choose our government." He calls it vote reparations.

≫ **"Say No to 'Anti-Racist' Racial Segregation in Schools"[8]**
The article brings awareness to the practice of "racial affinity spaces" in schools. "Affinity spaces involve schools encouraging students or staff to separate into segregated, race-based groups…. In all this, the "anti-racists" seem comfortable resurrecting practices clearly at odds

5   Joel Pollack, "Chicago's Art Institute Fires All of Its Docents: Too Many Wealthy White Ladies," Breitbart, October 16, 2021, https://www.breitbart.com/politics/2021/10/16/chicagos-art-institute-fires-all-docents-too-many-wealthy-white-ladies/.

6   Kathleen Anderson, "San Francisco Company Twilio Announces 'Anti-Racist' Layoff Policy," The Political Insider, September 19, 2022, https://thepoliticalinsider.com/san-francisco-company-twilio-announces-anti-racist-layoff-policy/.

7   Brandon Hasbrouck, "The Votes of Black Americans Should Count Twice," The Nation, December 17, 2020, https://www.thenation.com/article/society/black-votes-reparations-gerrymandering/.

8   Frederick Hess, "Say No to 'Anti-Racist' Racial Segregation in Schools," National Review, August 12, 2021, https://www.nationalreview.com/2021/08/say-no-to-anti-racist-racial-segregation-in-schools/.

with the 1964 Civil Rights Act." That's a policy the KKK could really get behind.

This could be continued seemingly endlessly. And it's not by accident. This is what Neo-Marxism purposely seeks to do. To pit one group of people against another, causing division, conflict, revolution, societal collapse, and then a new order. For the neo-Marxist offshoot CRT, division and discrimination are the name of the game. Ibram X. Kendi says as much in his book *How to Be an Antiracist,*

> "The only remedy to racist discrimination is **antiracist discrimination.** The only remedy to past discrimination is **present discrimination.** The only remedy to present discrimination is future discrimination."[9]

But I thought CRT says discrimination is bad (of course biblically we know it's wrong and why). So, if discrimination was wrong in the past wouldn't it be wrong in the present and future as well? CRT also says it was past discrimination that has led to so many of today's problems. So why would present and future discrimination lead to good solutions? For Kendi, it appears that discrimination is not inherently bad or wrong. It is just a tool that he would like to use in the present and future for outcomes

---

9   Ibram X. Kendi, *How to Be an Antiracist* (New York, NY: One World, 2019), p. 19.

he approves of. For the goals of CRT to be accomplished, discrimination is required.

Friends, CRT is also spelled DEI, and racism is also spelled CRT. Please be aware, as more light is shed on the true nature of CRT ideology, the more its practitioners avoid its name. Instead, they commonly use virtuous sounding titles like "anti-racism" and "DEI" to transmit their philosophical virus. But no matter what it is called, it is still partiality manifest. Critical race theorists practice real racism hoping to combat presumed, theoretical systemic racism. Applied CRT is racism declared as justice. This is the anti-justice of woke justice. The sin of partiality paraded as noble discrimination. Again, God tells us in James 2:9 (and in many other places),

> *But if you show partiality, you are committing sin and are convicted by the law as transgressors.*

Like all sins, this sin comes with a high cost. Akin to the old adage that clinging to bitterness is like drinking poison hoping it makes your foe sick, Virgil Walker declares,

> "CRT is a dangerous game … it actually destroys those it claims to help. It cries racism while clinging tightly to the same racist hatred it claims to despise and hopes to eliminate."[10]

The penance for all whites, for the sin of being white, is to always do the work of anti-racism. Regardless of an individual's history, attitudes, or actions. As Pastor Keller told us earlier, all whites are "involved in injustice" by the mere fact of having white skin and are "part of the problem." Sadly, the number of voices in Christian spaces echoing this same CRT sentiment could fill volumes.[11] Once again, this is the unbiblical idea of guilt by association or generational guilt. And once again, God's Word speaks directly to this,

---

10   Virgil Walker, "Episode 108 Critical Race Theory," "Just Thinking Podcast," start at 2:14:52, February 23, 2021, https://justthinking.me/ep-108-critical-race-theory/.

11   Two quick examples: Jemar Tisby's *The Color of Compromise* and Latasha Morrison's *Be the Bridge: Pursuing God's Heart for Racial Reconciliation*, are very popular in evangelical circles but are rich with CRT ideology.

The one who sins is the one who will die. The child will not share the guilt of the parent, nor will the parent share the guilt of the child (Ezekiel 18:20).

For the Son of Man is going to come with his angels in the glory of his Father, and then he will repay each person according to what he has done (Matthew 16:27).

He will render to each one according to his works (Romans 2:6).

This idea of generational, imputed guilt based on skin shade is anti-biblical, anti-gospel, and racist. But this is CRT's racist justice. CRT sweepingly proclaims all whites as guilty for historical sins and present-day systemic racism, therefore all whites must be about the work of anti-racism. Since the guilt is innate in whites, so is the responsibility. Darrell Harrison puts it like this,

> "But what critical race theory endeavors to do is to resurrect and re-prosecute those historical sins and leverage them in such a way as to hold white people hostage until they submit and acquiesce to their own set of sinfully prejudicial rules and decrees which apply exclusively to white people."[12]

And the work of anti-racism is never done. For whites there is no end, atonement, or forgiveness. As we heard from Ashleigh Shackelford earlier, whites are "always going to be racist." If you're white you have an incurable disease that demands unceasing works as treatment. Anti-racism is perpetual penance, a treadmill you can't get off of. And I don't know about you, but I hate treadmills. If you're white, your light brown skin has accrued a debt you can never pay off. All you can hope to do is to pay the interest on the debt, that is all the endless toil of anti-racism can accomplish. The minute you stop doing the work and paying the interest, the debt is called, and you are foreclosed on.

---

12 Darrell Harrison, "Episode 108 Critical Race Theory," *Just Thinking Podcast,* start at 2:10:23, February 23, 2021, https://justthinking.me/ep-108-critical-race-theory/.

Of utmost importance, when this pagan ideology is brought into the church, it audaciously proclaims the gospel is not enough. The gospel is not sufficient for the task of reconciliation. If you want that you must agree with CRT and apply its remedy. Because of this thinking, some CRT-inclined Christians go to the extent of calling the "reconciliation work" of anti-racism a salvation/gospel issue. Most egregiously, CRT says the gospel is not sufficient in salvation. Critical race theory cries out that Christ was wrong on the Cross when He said, "It is finished." For oppressive whites it is never finished, there is always more they must do for their sin of being white. CRT asserts that Christ's shed blood on the Cross is not enough to cover the sins of whites and make them truly new. For white Christians to overcome their stain of oppression they must add to their faith the doctrines of CRT and the continuous works of anti-racism. Do not miss this — the glorious gospel message of Christ's perfect life, atoning death, and victorious Resurrection, is not enough for CRT. More must be done, works must be added, the Cross is insufficient. Consequently, CRT is utterly anti-biblical and irredeemably anti-gospel; this is something we need to hear loud and clear! The true biblical gospel proclaims,

> *For by grace you have been saved through faith. And this is not your own doing; it is the gift of God, not a result of works, so that no one may boast (Ephesians 2:8–9).*

And once we have repented of our sins, put our faith in Christ, and have become new creations, Scripture assures us,

> There is therefore now **no condemnation** for **those** who are **in Christ Jesus** (Romans 8:1, emphasis added).

> as far as the east is from the west, so far does he remove our transgressions from us (Psalm 103:12).

> For I will be merciful toward their iniquities, and I will **remember their sins no more** (Hebrews 8:12, emphasis added).

That is good news indeed. But CRT and the woke mob always remembers. If you're not actively doing your penance of anti-racism, you're condemned already. And what is the goal of all this work of anti-racism? Socialism … I mean equity.

13

Equity

If you look up the meaning of the word "equity," you'll find definitions like "the quality of being fair or impartial."[1] You'll also find synonyms such as "justice, fairness, integrity."[2] Like the initial thoughts usually attached to the term "anti-racism," who wants to be found in opposition to these ideals? But just as "anti-racism" does not mean what you think it means in the CRT context, the same goes for "equity." Many tend to equate "equity" with "equality," but this is just not the case in the world of critical race theory. Here's the definition of "equity" in the CRT framework along with its distinction from "equality":

Equity: the demand for equal outcomes for groups regardless of any factors

Equality: everyone is viewed with equal value and given equal opportunities

Equality ascribes equal worth to every person and seeks to give all people the same opportunities to live, succeed, and flourish. As seen in the previous chapter, CRT does not want equality. It does not view all people as equals — the oppressors are guilty and inferior — nor does it want equal opportunities for all. The whole point of applied "anti-racism" and most "DEI" initiatives is to shift societal opportunities to the oppressed, to shift the balance of power. In fact, critical theorists argue it's impossible for all people to be treated equally in a fraudulent society engineered to advantage the oppressors. More on this in a moment. CRT wants equity, equal outcomes with no exclusions or excuses. In CRT thinking, this is "justice" and "fairness" because it is redistributing stolen power to the

---

1   https://www.dictionary.com/browse/equity.
2   https://www.thesaurus.com/browse/equity.

oppressed. As the stars of Disney's rebooted cartoon show *Proud Family* vigorously sang in a song performed for their middle school,

> "Slaves built this country; the descendants of slaves continue to build it…. And we the descendants of slaves in America have earned reparations for their suffering. And continue to earn reparations every moment we spend submerged in the systemic prejudice, racism, and white supremacy that America was founded with and still has not atoned for."[3]

Don't you want your kids watching that show? Unsurprisingly, it is the government's "righteous" responsibility to ensure this reparational reallocation and equitable outcome. This is socialism 101.

Equity in CRT is like Upwards Basketball. My son Ian has played in Upwards basketball for the last few years and has thoroughly enjoyed it. And I can unequivocally say, without any bias whatsoever, he is one of the best players. In Upwards basketball, they take kids at all skill levels within an age range and try to divide the talent up equally among different teams. Throughout the season each player gets equal playing time with everyone receiving the same award at the end. Neither the quality of the individual's play or the team's record matters. Everybody gets the same trophy; everybody gets the same outcome. This is equity. Don't misunderstand, I'm not picking on Upwards. It has been wonderful and done exactly what it's meant to do. It introduced my son to structured basketball and teamwork, giving him training, practice, and experience with a Christ-centered focus. I only use the analogy to drive home what equity means in CRT.

You can also think of it this way. Equality is like having a race, and each participant is ensured the same genuine starting point and given an equal opportunity to succeed. Of course, the results will be varied according to multiple factors, but the opportunity for all is the same. CRT's equity

---

3   Kendall Tietz, "Disney Slammed for 'Anti-White Propaganda' in New 'The Proud Family' Reboot," Fox News, February 6, 2023, https://www.foxnews.com/media/disney-slammed-anti-white-propaganda-proud-family-reboot.

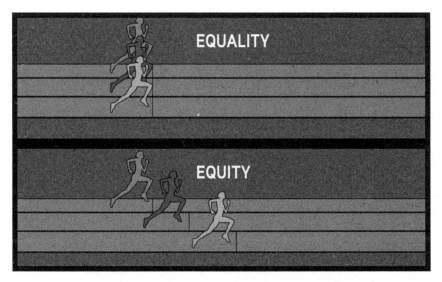

rejects this and says the starting line for the different participants must be adjusted to ensure everyone finishes at the same time.

As seen earlier, CRT dogmatically asserts that any unequal outcome between groups that is negative toward the oppressed is racism. Critical theorists flat out assume that equality is unimaginable in America because of the white privilege that allocates all true opportunities for success to whites alone. Any supposed opportunities for blacks in this rigged system is just more systemic oppression in disguise.[4] The oppression is so deep and protracted; CRT declares it is impossible to give blacks a fair starting point and a fair race. They've been victimized for too long. Therefore, as Ibram X. Kendi said,

> "The only remedy to racist discrimination is antiracist discrimination. The only remedy to past discrimination is present discrimination. The only remedy to present discrimination is future discrimination."[5]

---

4   This can often take the form of the "no true Scotsman" logical fallacy. In short, this is when someone changes the definition of keywords in an argument to validate their point. In this case the word opportunity is redefined. In CRT thinking, any opportunity the oppressed receive is not a real opportunity, and everything is still oppression.

5   Ibram X. Kendi, *How to Be an Antiracist* (New York, NY: One World, 2019), p. 19.

As a comprehensive worldview, CRT assumes systemic racism, interprets diverse outcomes as racist, declares this as proof of inequality, and demands its version of equity. This ultimately means the government must forcibly intervene to reallocate societal resources and opportunities to the oppressed in the name of justice. In all this, systemic oppression is the only problem, whites are the lone guilty party, discriminatory redistribution of wealth and power the only answer.

It cannot be overstated that all of this is arbitrarily assumed and concluded within the pagan Neo-Marxist paradigm. As such, it fundamentally rejects biblical categories at every level. People are identified by groups instead of individuals made in God's image. The only sin is oppression and only the oppressors are guilty, instead of the biblical reality that all are guilty sinners. Salvation is found in coercive redistribution and revolution, not through the gospel of Jesus Christ in the individual heart. CRT's focus on group identity and the guiltlessness of the oppressed utterly dismisses the biblical truth of personal accountability. The Bible repeatedly states that God will "render to each one according to his works" (Romans 2:6). Biblically, every person is accountable for (1) their own sin before God and (2) for how they steward their God-given gifts and opportunities. Not only that, but Scripture is also clear that individuals face the consequences of their choices.

> *For according to the work of a man he will repay him,*
> *and according to his ways he will make it befall him*
> *(Job 34:11).*

The NIV translation says, *"he brings on them what their conduct deserves."* Accountability for one's own actions is biblically unavoidable. But CRT's definition of identity assigned by group, and the individuals default guilt or innocence based on their group, has absolutely no room for this. The attitudes, words, choices, or actions of the individuals in both groups are completely inconsequential. All disparities are racism, all oppressors are to blame, all the oppressed are victims. The CRT dye has been cast and discriminatory redistribution is the lone answer. God's Word has a much different assessment and a very different answer.

This is not to say that the answer to societal problems or disparities is just "pull yourself up by your bootstraps." It's also not being claimed that poverty is not complicated or that genuine injustices do not presently exist. A plethora of factors can reinforce cycles of poverty, and injustices abound in a society filled with unjust sinners. It is to say that dismissing biblical principles for individuals and society in favor of a destructive pagan ideology, will never be the answer. CRT puts its faith in the wrong foundational authority and consequently is severely incorrect about people, society, their problems, and the solution. Being flatly opposed to the Bible, the only source of truth that is sufficient to address every issue, is what makes CRT so disastrously wrong. Any proposed societal resolution that abandons God's revealed Word in favor of sinful man's fallible ideas, like CRT, is inherently flawed and bound for failure.

Nonetheless, it's not hard to understand the appeal of some of CRT's ideas to unsuspecting Christians. The language is so familiar and therefore persuasive. CRT's narrative of combatting injustice, helping the oppressed, fighting racism, fairness and equity resonates with Christians because it's borrowed biblical language. Indeed, Scripture calls Christians to seek justice, help the downtrodden, and show no partiality (Isaiah 1:17, Deuteronomy 1:17). But as we've continually seen, CRT may employ familiar biblical vocabulary, but it is using a completely different

dictionary. Often, its definitions and underlying meanings are completely contradictory to biblical understanding and application. This is one of the primary reasons why CRT is so deceptive and dangerous.

Some professing believers even go to the extent of claiming CRT is right because the Bible, and Jesus, teach a form of socialism. As "proof," they point to many different biblical passages that are typically taken out of context or are just misunderstood. For example, they claim the Bible's repeated commands to provide for the needy is socialistic. But those commands are for individuals to give voluntarily out of generosity, not government-forced redistribution. Private property for the owner was assumed and equal outcomes for all was not demanded. The early New Testament church is also often proclaimed as a form of socialism because,

> *There was not a needy person among them, for as many as*
> *were owners of lands or houses sold them and brought the*
> *proceeds of what was sold and laid it at the apostles' feet,*
> *and it was distributed to each as any had need*
> *(Acts 4:34–35).*

But again, this was completely voluntary, not mandated or coerced by a ruling body. It is a vivid example of the type of generosity that should be inspired by a common love for Christ and His bride, the Church. The

Equity

Bible says give, CRT says take. One is love and kindness, the other, a form of partiality and theft. No, the Bible does not advocate for socialism.

Christians sympathetic to CRT and socialism often make the argument that Jesus was the original social justice warrior. He associated with the marginalized, rebuked privileged abusive religious leaders, took care of the needy, and proclaimed liberation for the oppressed. And no doubt, He did all those things. Just not in the way they think or for the socialistic goals they have. When Jesus engaged the marginalized of society, He didn't tell them they were innocent and needed to revolt against oppression to achieve equity. He told them to repent of their sin and believe in Him alone for salvation. This is the same admonition Jesus gave to the religious leaders He so often sternly rebuked for their hypocrisy, pride, and abuse. The problem for both groups was sin, the answer for all is repentance and faith in Christ.[6] And no doubt, Jesus ministered to the needy with teaching, miracles, and healings. But this same ministry was offered to the wealthy and privileged of society as well. For example, Jesus taught in Zacchaeus' house, healed the servant of a Roman centurion, and healed an official's son (Luke 19:1–10, Luke 7:1–10, John 4:43–54). The point of all these things was to fulfill prophecy and to confirm His identity to all as the long-awaited Savior Messiah.

The account of Jesus and the "rich young ruler" is also presented as support for the idea that Jesus was pro-socialism. Yes, Jesus did tell the rich young man to "go, sell what you possess and give to the poor, and you will have treasure in heaven; and come, follow me" (Matthew 19:16–22). But in context, Jesus did not give him this instruction to make amends for his privilege or to earn societal salvation. It appears that Jesus was revealing to the young man his idolatry of wealth and need to forsake all and follow Christ. Also, there were a lot of rich people Jesus interacted with and did not tell to give their wealth away. Jesus' message to all was the same, turn away from your sin and put your faith in Him alone for salvation. Jesus, God who became flesh, showed no partiality, and stands in direct conflict

---

6   A great example of this is Jesus' conversations with Nicodemus and the Samaritan woman in John 3 and 4.

with Neo-Marxist CRT, which demands partiality toward the designated oppressed.

Jesus' care for people's earthly needs is undeniable. But there is nothing in His teachings or ministry that infers, much less demands, the necessity for equal societal and economic outcomes for every individual. Also, the fact that Jesus didn't call for, or lead, a revolution against tyrannically oppressive Rome, is further evidence He wasn't a social justice warrior. Jesus' primary concern was the liberation of the oppressed from the systemic oppression of sin. Every human is born under the bondage, the oppression of sin, and every image bearer's ultimate need is to be set free from that slavery. CRT proclaims that salvation comes to a society when cultural power is shifted from the oppressors to the oppressed. Jesus, and all of Scripture, definitively declares that salvation for each individual can only be found in Christ alone. No, Jesus was not a social justice/equity warrior.

Moving on, CRT's understanding of equity does not align with reality or Scripture. How exactly do you guarantee equal outcomes for every person, in every situation, with such incomprehensible variation in people and societal factors? It never works out in practice in the real world, as every society who has ever tried socialism could testify. And don't tell anyone, but this is why we kept track of Ian's points and the team's record in Upwards basketball. To prepare him for real basketball and the real world where varying outcomes is the norm. More importantly, God's Word rejects the concept of equity as proposed by critical race theorists.

By CRT standards, God is unjust and inequitable, and His creation proves it. Scripture emphatically states that *"by him all things were created ... all things were created through him and for him" (Colossians 1:16).* And in His creation, it is abundantly evident that God loves variation and diversity, including in humans. Within the mind-boggling variety of humanity, God is perfectly fine with some people having more or less of any number of things. Some people have more height than others, some have more melanin, some have more intelligence, some have more musical ability, others are more athletically gifted. Some are better with finances, some are better mechanically, some have more rhythm, some have more hair than others, and you get the idea. All of this is not just okay with God, but it is good in His eyes. To be clear, it is the diversity ingrained by God's design within humanity, such as differing talents and genetics, which glorifies God. Any "diversity" that diverts from God's creation ordinances and revealed will for how we are designed (such as homosexual "marriage") does not glorify God. The rejection of God's design and commands is not "diversity," it is sinful rebellion. God, our Designer and Creator is only pleased and glorified by the diversity that He built into us and commanded for us. That said, humanity's designed diversity glorifies our Maker, and each unique human equally displays the image of God and is equal in value. Biblically, variation and varying outcomes is not necessarily injustice.

What God measures, and holds every individual accountable to, is each person's faithfulness in their God-given opportunities. A good example of this is the parable of the talents found in Matthew 25:14–30. In that parable, the master of the house gave three of his servants different amounts of talents (money) to steward while he was gone. When he returned, he judged each one according to their faithfulness, not by their outcomes, compared one to another. He did not scold the servant who gained three more talents for not getting five more like the other servant. The servant who was judged wasn't condemned because he had less to start with or because he didn't produce five or three more talents like the other two servants. He was rightly condemned because he was not faithful with the one talent he was given. God measures our faithfulness, not our outcomes; this is the focus of God's justice and judgment. And every person has an equal opportunity to be faithful with what God has given, whatever the amount or circumstances may be.[7]

---

7   Some may argue that the parable in Matthew 20:1–16 of the workers hired at different times but receiving the same wages is an example of equal outcomes. But parables tend to make one major point. And this one is bringing home the reality that the master, representing God, has the right to do what He wants with His own resources. This parable actually affirms private property as it shows the master doing as He pleases with His own money. And in no way is it ever implied that the master was required to pay each worker the same wage.

CRT's quest for "equity" typically involves a form of theft and possibly covetousness (Exodus 20:15, 17). To accomplish their goals, critical race theorists are all about creating unequal scales to rig the outcome to their desired end. The Bible emphatically and repeatedly lets us know that God hates unequal, unjust scales.

> *Unequal weights and unequal measures are both alike an abomination to the Lord (Proverbs 20:10).*

> *You shall do no wrong in judgment, in measures of length or weight or quantity (Leviticus 19:35).*

> *A false balance is an abomination to the Lord, but a just weight is his delight (Proverbs 11:1).*

In CRT, the end justifies the means. Not so with Christianity. God cares about the "means" and He controls the "end." Christians are commanded to do God's will God's way and leave the outcomes in His perfectly just hands.

There may be a lot of shared language between the Bible and CRT, but the definitions are usually as different as night and day. If we're not careful, it's all too easy to be ensnared by *"deceptive philosophy which depends on human tradition … rather than on Christ" (Colossians 2:8; NIV)*. As Christians, let's be sure we are defining our terms and our lives by the Word of God and not the opinions of men.

Is the Social Justice Movement Biblical?

14

For many people this is the big question, and the short answer is no, no, and no. In actuality, it is pervasively anti-biblical. Some might find this answer quite shocking because how can something called "social justice" be antithetical to the Bible? Well, as we've seen time and again, how terms are defined makes all the difference. And the modern social justice movement is essentially defined by critical theorists within the worldview of Neo-Marxism. Today's social justice crusade is CRT forcibly applied to our cultural context. In fact, since social justice is born out of CRT, many of its own advocates often call it "Critical Social Justice" (CSJ)[1] to emphasize its origin and purpose. For this reason, I will often refer to social justice as CSJ. With that key background information in place, let's do the ever-important task of defining our terms. What is the modern secular notion of CSJ according to its architects and leaders?

Critical Social Justice: 1. The quest for equity in terms of distribution of wealth, opportunities, privileges, and power for groups within society. 2. As a movement, it seeks to identify the oppressed and to right societal wrongs through the redistribution of power and resources.

The Oxford Dictionary gives a similar definition to social justice as provided above and then says to see "distributive justice,"[2] literally meaning to redistribute wealth and influence to oppressed groups. Social Justice is state redistribution driven by politics and power that seeks to combat and ultimately replace society's rigged and unjust power structures. And

---

1   One example, in this article DiAngelo and Sensoy argue that "Critical Social Justice Pedagogy" is CRT ideology fleshed out in the teaching of "social justice." O. Sensoy, R. DiAngelo (2014). Respect Differences? Challenging the Common Guidelines in Social Justice Education. Democracy and Education, 22 (2), Article 1, https://democracyeducationjournal.org/home/vol22/iss2/1.

2   https://www.oed.com/dictionary/social-justice_n?tab=meaning_and_use&hide-all-quotations=true#132635088100.

with the CRT understanding of equity as its goal, when you hear "social justice," just think socialism. Calling something "justice" doesn't make it so. As discussed in the last chapter, socialism is a form of coveting, theft, and unequal scales, all of which are detested by God and oppose biblical justice.

A key component of CSJ is to identify the oppressed and even their level of oppression. This is where the term "intersectionality" comes into play. Remember from chapter three that intersectionality is a tool used by the CSJ warrior to determine who's oppressed, by how much, and thus appropriate reparation. It's the idea that there are multiple layers of cultural oppression that can intersect and compound, dramatically increasing oppression. Though there are more, critical theorists generally classify these attributes as oppressive: white, male, heterosexual, cisgender, able-bodied, colonialists, Christian. The oppressed, to one degree or another, are those who do not match those attributes: non-whites, non-males, non-heterosexuals, non-binary/transgender, disabled, indigenous, non-Christian. The more victim groups a person checks off, the greater their oppression, and the more redistributed societal power and wealth they deserve. All of this is based on CRT's arbitrarily assigned identity groups with presumed guilt or innocence. And what is one of the primary methods CSJ employs to "right" all this oppression? Diversity, Equity, and Inclusion. **Diverse** (non-oppressor) groups must be **included** (often by excluding oppressors) in societal opportunities and influence to achieve **equity** (redistribution). Don't forget that CRT is also spelled DEI.

Dear Christian, please note that CRT/CSJ views Christianity itself as a major cultural oppressor. Biblical Christianity is considered the white man's religion and a foundational pillar of systemic oppression. This is believed despite the fact that Christianity flourished in the Middle East, Southwest Asia, and Northern Africa long before taking root in Europe or America. Christianity's doctrines of marriage, gender, gender roles, sexuality, family, and so on, are seen as institutions of the hegemony that maintain the oppressive status quo. The historical Christian threads that make up so much of America's societal fabric are seen as a web of oppression that only benefits the oppressors. If that wasn't bad enough, Christianity unifies all of humanity in value, sinfulness, and need of salvation found in Christ alone. This is entirely loathsome and unacceptable for CRT and the CSJ warrior. If we stopped here, it would be enough to definitively demonstrate that CSJ is not biblical or, as some put it, "a gospel issue." But wait, there's more.

Critical theory is a long train. The issue of race and "racial reconciliation," CRT, is just one boxcar on that train.[3] Attached to the critical theory engine you'll also find the boxcars of feminism, LGBTQIA2S+, transgenderism, global justice/redistribution, and even climate justice. There are more and surely others will be added. All these movements and agendas are driven by the same Neo-Marxist ideology of oppressor versus oppressed; oppression is systemic, power and resources must be redistributed. Critical theorists endeavor to create and recruit as many victimized groups as possible in order to destabilize, divide, and conquer a society. All in the name of justice. This idea is concisely stated by four premier critical race theorists who co-authored the book *Words that Wound,* from which we quoted earlier,

> "Critical race theory works toward the end of eliminating racial
> oppression as a part of the broader goal of ending all forms of

---

3   The analogy of critical theory as a train is not original to me. I've seen it used multiple times from different speakers and authors. If I knew who used it first I would give them due credit.

oppression. Racial oppression is experienced by many in tandem with oppression on grounds of gender, class, or sexual orientation."[4]

CRT is just the tip of the Neo-Marxist iceberg. Their stated goal is to end all forms of oppression, oppression which Neo-Marxists typically associate with biblical norms and doctrines. That's why Black Lives Matter, an organization run by self-professed Marxists, said on their website "We disrupt the Western-prescribed nuclear family" and "dismantle the patriarchal practice." These statements were on a page on their website, called "What We Believe," which was promptly taken down after intense public backlash.[5]

Probably the most vivid example of this is the current LGBTQ/transgender revolution sweeping through America. If you listen closely, you will hear the creed of critical theory all throughout this movement's propaganda. The argument goes like this — heterosexuality, marriage, and the nuclear family are societal institutions that are systemically oppressive, established by the oppressors to entrench their dominance and for their ongoing cultural advantage.[6] Sexual minorities, those who don't conform to heterosexuality in any number of ways, have long endured, and continue to endure, harsh, unjust, detrimental oppression. Therefore, they are due reparations. Cultural power, privilege, authority, and resources must be reallocated to this oppressed group. They are to be given cultural influence in every way possible, and their enlightened oppressed voices are to be followed without question. All that they do to shift cultural power from the oppressors to themselves and other oppressed groups is right and good. Any call for them to repent of their sin is just oppressive "white" Christianity (again, Christians who compromise with CRT

---

4   Mari J Matsuda, Charles R. Lawrence III, Richard Delgado, Kimberle Williams Crenshaw, *Words That Wound: Critical Race Theory, Assaultive MiSpeech, And The First Amendment* (New York, NY: Routledge, 2018), p. 6.

5   Anthony Leonardi, "Black Lives Matter 'What We Believe' page that includes disrupting 'nuclear family structure' removed from website," *Washington Examiner,* September 21, 2020, https://www.washingtonexaminer.com/news/1900774/black-lives-matter-what-we-believe-page-that-includes-disrupting-nuclear-family-structure-removed-from-website/.

6   Here's an example. Harris Rigby, George Mason professor, says marriage promotes "White heteropatriarchal supremacy," Not the Bee, March 18, 2024, https://notthebee.com/article/professor-says-marriage-promotes-white-supremacy.

eventually must compromise the gospel). If you disagree, question, or simply do not celebrate the movement, you are a hateful, oppressive bigot who is part of the problem. Sound familiar? If you've been wondering why the excessive societal push to exalt LGBTQ voices and to give them unrestrained cultural authority, this is the answer. The LGBTQ agenda is calling its plays straight from the Neo-Marxist, critical theory playbook. The LGBTQ/transgender revolution is just another boxcar being pulled along at high speeds by the critical theory locomotive.

As an aside, one must wonder how the LGBTQ group can still call themselves oppressed with all the social power they wield. They have almost complete control of the cultural megaphone and bully pulpit. The alphabet mafia has seemingly unfettered influence on media, entertainment, education, corporations, and governmental institutions. How exactly are they oppressed? But I guess all of that is deserved reparation and a useful tool in the critical theorist's hand to deconstruct society.

Back to the critical theory train. This is what seems to happen to many Christians. They will jump on the social justice/CRT boxcar out of a sincere desire for justice and in ignorance of the anti-biblical worldview driving the movement. When they initially jumped on, they had no intention of supporting Neo-Marxism or the other boxcars of feminism, LGBTQ revolution, climate justice, etc. They had an earnest desire to

love people, promote racial reconciliation, and obey God's command to seek justice. But unbeknownst to them, by jumping on that boxcar they attached themselves to the whole critical theory train that demands one biblical compromise after another, being carried along by an ideology that seeks to dismantle biblical cultural influence in the name of justice and liberation.

And of course, the Christian's desire for justice and reconciliation is unquestionably good and right. Tragically, injustices have permeated humanity since Genesis 3. They are the heartbreaking, temporary consequences of living in a sin-cursed world that Christ will completely destroy when He returns. Christians are called to ease the effects of sin by practicing the love of Christ, providing for those in need, and defending the weak. Most importantly, believers have been commissioned to point all people to Christ, our only true hope for now and eternity. By doing these things, Christians are salt and light to a decaying and dark world. Believers in Christ should be, and typically are, leading the charge against partiality and oppression because we have been commanded to do justice.

> *He has told you, O man, what is good; and what does the*
> *Lord require of you but to do justice, and to love kindness,*
> *and to walk humbly with your God? (Micah 6:8).*

We are to love justice because our God loves justice.

> *He loves righteousness and justice; the earth is full of the*
> *steadfast love of the Lord (Psalm 33:5).*

Christians are commanded to judge justly, showing no partiality toward anyone, the poor or the rich.

> *You shall do no injustice in court. You shall not be partial*
> *to the poor or defer to the great, but in righteousness shall*
> *you judge your neighbor (Leviticus 19:15).*

This all leads to the primary question of who defines justice? As stated in the first chapter of this book, foundationally there are only two options: either it's God or man. There is no neutral ground to be found, either you put your faith in God's Word or in man's ideas. Everyone must choose which authority they will bow to. Ultimately, man's attempts to define justice are arbitrary because, apart from God, there is no absolute authority or standard to hold everyone accountable to. Only the one, true, and living God rightly defines justice both now and forever. And when we look in His Word, justice never has an adjective in front of it. Biblically, there are no variations of justice. There is simply justice and injustice. What things are just? Things in line with God's Word, God's law, and God's nature. What things are unjust? Things not in line with God's Word, law, and nature. Thus, justice is repeatedly defined like this throughout Scripture,

> *Thus says the Lord of hosts, Render true judgments, show*
> *kindness and mercy to one another, do not oppress the*
> *widow, the fatherless, the sojourner, or the poor, and let*
> *none of you devise evil against another in your heart*
> *(Zechariah 7:9–10).*

> *These are the things that you shall do: Speak the truth*
> *to one another; render in your gates judgments that are*
> *true and make for peace; do not devise evil in your hearts*

against one another, and love no false oath, for all these
things I hate, declares the Lord (Zechariah 8:16–17).

Justice is inextricably tied to God's righteousness and character. Fundamentally, justice exists because there's a just God who's the unchanging source and standard of morality. Injustice exists because people are sinners, in rebellion against their Creator. And people can recognize injustice because they're made in God's image.

When you boil down the CSJ movement, its definition of "justice" is state redistribution of societal goods through power and politics. To do this it practices extreme partiality and the prejudicial judgment of people in accordance with their identity group. This is not biblical justice. Scripture is clear there is to be no partiality and each person is judged individually according to their deeds (James 2:1, Deuteronomy 24:16, Jeremiah 31:30, Matthew 16:27). Biblical justice is all about obedience to God's law and a heart that willingly submits. Woke justice is a power issue, biblical justice is a heart issue. Christians are undoubtedly to seek justice, but real justice requires truth, which is only found in God and His Word. Therefore, believers in Christ are to seek biblical justice and reconciliation using biblical presuppositions, categories, and means. We do not seek equal outcomes, rather righteous obedience, trusting God with both the process and the results. This is summarized well by Darrell Harrison,

> "The definition of true justice is grounded in God's Word and … as we the people of God advocate for true justice — within that objective biblical definition, a definition that is without partiality, bias, or prejudice — we are not to sin ourselves in the pursuit of it. Now when you look closely at critical race theory, you'll see clearly that it violates both of those principles. Which is precisely why believers in Jesus Christ must reject it."[7]

And what is the heartbeat of God's justice? That *"all have sinned and fall short of the glory of God" (Romans 3:23).* By God's perfect standard we

---

7   Darrell Harrison, Episode 108 "Critical Race Theory," *Just Thinking* Podcast, start at 3:20:28, February 23, 2021, https://justthinking.me/ep-108-critical-race-theory/.

are all unjust and undone! All have egregiously violated God's law, and all are justly accountable to His absolute justice. No exceptions. This is God's justice and the Christian's primary concern. CRT and CSJ are ambiguous, racist, man-centered ideas. Arbitrarily declaring who's to blame and who's owed, who's the oppressor and who's the oppressed, based on skin shade and identity group. Their basic message is the oppressed are owed and deserve compensation. But God's justice says that we're all to blame and we all deserve death! Only God is just, and He will judge the unjust. That's you, me, and everyone else.

> *For whoever keeps the whole law but fails in one point has become guilty of all of it (James 2:10).*

> *For the wages of sin is death (Romans 6:23a).*

> *because he has fixed a day on which he will judge the world in righteousness by a man whom he has appointed; and of this he has given assurance to all by raising him from the dead (Acts 17:31).*

How can we survive God's perfect, eternal, righteous justice? By repenting of our sin, putting our faith in Christ, the God who left His privilege to purchase our salvation by making reparation for all our sin (Romans 5:8, Acts 17:30, Romans 10:9). **This** is the gospel! This is God's justice.

This was the focus of Jesus' earthly ministry. And as we rightly strive for biblical justice on earth, there is something we must remember. If someone could right every injustice, it would not buy them one drop of blood from Calvary or earn them a single second in heaven. Salvation is through Christ alone! This is the gospel message and the focus of biblical justice.

Friends, the woke justice of the CSJ movement literally gets every core issue wrong. In assuming group identity, oppression as the only sin, redistribution/revolution as the answer, CSJ is catastrophically mistaken about man's identity, problem, and required solution. The reality of the unity that Christianity brings to mankind in equality of value, sinfulness, and gospel need is anathema to CSJ. Critical race theory detests this unity because of its lust for cultural power, division, deconstruction, revolution, and the exaltation of humanity. These two worldviews could not be more different.

No, the modern social justice movement is not biblical nor is it "part of the gospel." Woke justice is injustice. It is an anti-biblical ideology that is utterly impotent against actual racism. Worse than that, it manufactures and fuels racist discrimination in the name of justice. So, if CRT isn't the answer to racism, what is? Glad you asked.

15

The Only Answer to Racism and Reconciliation

The "conversations" in our culture today around the issues of racism and racial reconciliation seem endless. The dominant narrative on these topics coming from the "cultural elites," who have pervasive control over societal modes of communication, is anchored in CRT. Though they may not often use the words "critical race theory" or "Neo-Marxism," if you listen closely, you'll hear those ideas echoing loudly. The terms and definitions they use betray them and it is readily evident that their paradigm for racial problems and solutions is rooted in critical theory. As we've already seen, using CRT to deal with racism is like trying to put out a fire with gasoline. Those peddling these ideas, in full or in part, are either tragically deceived or maliciously purposeful. When Christians advocate for these ideas, it is doubly tragic. Not only are they pushing concepts that fuel racism and undermine the reconciliation they desperately seek, they do so while possessing the true answer.

As Christians we must realize that we have the answers to racism and reconciliation that our culture is clamoring for. The biblical framework alone, rooted in the real history of Genesis 1–11, gives the only right understanding of humanity's identity, problem, and solution. Only the Bible consistently establishes the inherent unchangeable equality of each unique human being. In Genesis 1:27 we read,

> *"So God created man in his own image, in the image of God he created him; male and female he created them."*

The image of God that was stamped onto Adam and Eve was inherited by all of their descendants, which is every human in history. This reminds us of the reality that there is only one human race and that all humans are of one blood (Acts 17:26, Malachi 2:10), a fact confirmed by real science

REPARATIONS INJUSTICES

as seen in chapter 4. Humanity's magnificent diversity only highlights our Creator's brilliant creativity and points us back to our amazing God in whose image each person is made. It is because of this biblical and historical truth that we are repeatedly commanded throughout Scripture to practice impartial love and justice for all (Deuteronomy 1:17, Matthew 22:37–40, James 2:1–9). But again, if everything just evolved after nothing exploded there's no reason for demanding impartiality or humanity's equality.

The Bible alone accounts for racism's origin and wickedness. The root cause for racism is sin and we see the origin of sin back in Genesis 3. After Adam and Eve sinned, their sin nature was then passed on to all their descendants. This is why every person, no matter their skin shade, is born sinful. We are all sinners by nature and subsequently by choice. And when you boil racism down to its core, what is it? Sin, the sin of pride. Racism (real racism, not CRT's agenda-driven redefinition) basically says, "I'm better than you." The reasons for this self-exaltation are legion and are found globally because the world is filled with sinful humans. As I've had the opportunity to travel around the world, I've been able to observe this firsthand. Despite what CRT would seemingly have you believe, racism isn't unique to America. Racism is a global problem that raises its ugly head in various manifestations. Different excuses are used, but it's the same essential sin. Someone's skin is too light or dark, they're from the wrong tribe or social class, and so on. Every person, in the pride of their sinful heart, can find countless reasons to elevate themselves and demean others. And racism in any form is wicked because it rejects God's assigned equality of every person and His command to honor each person accordingly.

It is only after rightly identifying the source of humanity's racism problem that the right solution be assigned. At its core, racism is not a societal power issue only plaguing a particular group identified by CRT as oppressors. Racism is an expression of the sin of pride and, like all sin, it is rebellion against the Creator and can affect anyone in any culture. Ultimately, racism is a sinful heart issue. This definitively means that racism's only true remedy is a changed heart through the gospel of Jesus Christ! Because, hear me, dear friend, despite what CRT would tell you, racism is not a skin issue, it is a sin issue. Salvation, found only in the Last Adam, is racism's sole cure (Ezekiel 36:26, 1 Corinthians 15:21–22, 2 Corinthians 5:17).

The secular humanism that currently dominates our cultural landscape vehemently rejects the biblical categories necessary to identify and address racism. Those who have embraced any variation of this creed are groping for answers in the dark on the wrong ideological planet. Christian, we've got the answer — the question is, what will we do with it?

Some will say, "But what about the injustices of the past, reparations, and reconciliation?" Here again, the gospel is the only genuine answer. As Christians, we can and must identify and condemn the injustices of the past for the horrific evils they were. We can also rightly acknowledge the multi-generational effects of those travesties. We are commanded to meet the real needs of our neighbors and to strive for biblical justice using biblical means, taking comfort in the fact that when Christ returns no injustice will escape His perfect justice. But all of this is to be done within the glorious eternal truth that everything has been paid for on the Cross. For believers in Christ, there is no sin that does not carry the stamp "paid in full." Their sin debt has been fully covered for all of eternity and they do not inherit the debt of any who came before them. When Jesus declared on the Cross, "It is finished," He meant it. With all this in mind, Christians are called to put off hostility and resentment and put on love and forgiveness. We are commissioned to joyfully forgive because we have been forgiven.

> "Let all bitterness and wrath and anger and clamor and slander be put away from you, along with all malice. Be kind to one another, tenderhearted, forgiving one another, as God in Christ forgave you" (Ephesians 4:31–32).

> "bearing with one another and, if one has a complaint against another, forgiving each other; as the Lord has forgiven you, so you also must forgive" (Colossians 3:13).

Of course this is utterly foreign to CRT, CSJ, and the cult of wokeism. Why? These Neo-Marxist atheist ideologies know nothing of God's justice, forgiveness, redemption, and salvation. All they know, preach, and require is division, animosity, retribution, and the unceasing works of anti-racism as perpetual penance. Not so for those in Christ. We are to be the forgiving people. Christians are to forgive in response to who God is, what He has done, and what He has commanded in His Word. It's hard to think of anything more oxymoronic than an "unforgiving Christian."

This attitude and practice of forgiveness is necessary for reconciliation. Truly, the reconciliation earnestly sought by so many resides only in the accomplished work of Christ. It is in Christ alone that forgiveness is found, animosity dies, and authentic unity is born.

> "But now in Christ Jesus you who once were far off have been brought near by the blood of Christ. For he himself is our peace, who has made us both one and has broken down in his flesh the dividing wall of hostility by abolishing the law of commandments expressed in ordinances, that he might create in himself one new man in place of the two, so making peace, and might reconcile us both to God in one body through the cross, thereby killing the hostility" (Ephesians 2:13–16).

*From now on, therefore, **we regard no one according to the flesh**. Even though we once regarded Christ according to the flesh, we regard Him thus no longer. Therefore, **if anyone is in Christ, he is a new creation.** The old has passed away; behold, the new has come (2 Corinthians 5:16–17, emphasis added).*

"There is neither Jew nor Greek, there is neither slave nor free, there is no male and female, for you are all one in Christ Jesus" (Galatians 3:28).

Praise God, Christians are new creations in Christ, born again into a new heavenly family with one Father. And in Christ there is neither slave nor free, black nor white, all are "one new man," reconciled to God and to each other. It is by the blood of Christ that division is destroyed, hostility is killed, and reconciliation is achieved. Owen Strachan says it well in his book *Christianity and Wokeness,*

> "God has not tried to reconcile us through the cross. Calvary is not His best shot at unification, with later needed boosts from Marxism and other ideologies. God has reconciled us through the cross."[1]

---

1   Owen Strachan, *Christianity and Wokeness: How the Social Justice Movement Is Hijacking the Gospel — and the Way to Stop It* (Washington, D.C. Salem Books, 2021) p. 163.

Does this mean that a person's ethnicity and cultural heritage should be disregarded as meaningless? Certainly not. God loves and is glorified by the variety He has fashioned within His creation, including in humanity. In Revelation 7:9–10 we are given a glimpse into heaven and the Author specifically draws attention to this divinely created diversity,

> "After this I looked, and behold, a **great multitude** that no one could number, **from every nation, from all tribes and peoples and languages,** standing before the throne and before the Lamb, clothed in white robes, with palm branches in their hands, and crying out with a loud voice, 'Salvation belongs to our **God** who sits on the throne, and to the Lamb!'" (emphasis mine).

We can all rejoice in the "nation" and "tribe" God sovereignly placed us in for His purposes and glory. Our ethnicity and heritage are part of who we are by God's design. But they, just like every other part of our identity, are subservient to, and are defined by, our ultimate identity found in Christ alone. For those who have put their faith in King Jesus, there is neither Jew nor Greek, just Christian. The result is magnificent diversity and eternal unity in the body of Christ. And in the midst of the dynamic division engulfing our culture, the Church can be a beacon of unity, a light in the divisive darkness.

As a final thought, allow me to share this as a cautionary tale. When you look at the history of slavery in America it is right to ask, where was the church? Now don't misunderstand, it was Christians, rooted in a biblical worldview, which led the charge to abolish slavery in America and throughout the west. But why didn't the church uniformly stand up to the culture of the time, renounce slavery and proclaim the equality of every person based on Scripture? Speaking broadly, I believe there were two primary reasons. One, many Christians had compromised, to one degree or another, with the culture's teaching about different people and their worth. Abandoning the clear teaching of the Bible, some would even twist Scripture to justify their unbiblical views. Two, many other Christians did not agree with the cultural narrative or practice of their day but chose not to engage. They lacked the answers, motivation, or the courage to confront the evil of their time. Christians and the church at large disengaged on the issue, left it to secularists and secular thinking, and you see what happened.

This should be a wakeup call for believers today. Dear Christian, we will never influence this culture for Christ by abandoning God's Word or by abandoning the culture. Rather, we lovingly confront this culture for Christ with the transforming truth of the Word of the living God. Only by boldly standing on Scripture can we effectively engage this culture and be the salt and light God has called us to be. There is only one answer to racism, and CRT is not it. Humanity's only real hope of redemption, reconciliation, and restoration is found in the Word and work of Christ alone. Christian, you have the answers so many are looking for. What will you do with them?

16

Fear Not, God's Word Is Forever Sufficient

Honestly, it is easy to see the allure of the CRT narrative to unsuspecting Christians. At first glance there appears to be so much overlap with Christianity with all the familiar words and concepts. Talk of justice, defending the weak, helping the oppressed, ending racism, and achieving societal reconciliation naturally resonates with believers in Christ. Christians have a plethora of biblical reasons and mandates, along with a God given love, to engage these issues. And who wants to be known for being on the side of the "oppressors," the "racists," and those causing multigenerational injustice? Anybody want to volunteer to be identified as against "anti-racism," or to seem to deny that black lives matter? On top of all that, CRT is deviously "slippery" because of how it manipulates words and arguments to turn any resistance into "proof" for racism. Add in America's past with all these things and it's understandable how Christians could be innocently deceived into sympathizing with CRT at first hearing.

That's why one of the primary purposes of this book is to pull back the veil of CRT to reveal its rotten anti-biblical worldview. Exposing its redefinitions, twisting of ideas, logical fallacies, and constant "baiting and switching" that ultimately seek to deceive and to destroy. That I might quote one of my favorite characters, Inigo Montoya, from one of my favorite movies, *The Princess Bride*, and say to misled Christians using CRT jargon,

> "You keep using that word. I do not think it means what you think it means."

As we've seen, this quote is ever so appropriate when dealing with critical race theory. CRT may use a lot of words common to Christians, but it has a completely different dictionary based on an entirely different authority.

In all its Neo-Marxist word play, CRT commits racism in the name of reconciliation and oppression in the name of liberation. The end result is plain to see to any honest observer, **woke justice advances injustice in the name of justice.**

Unfortunately, many Christians, likely with sincere motives, have bought what CRT is selling at some level. As demonstrated throughout the book, numerous believers are embracing the presuppositions, categories, terms, and definitions of CRT to varying degrees. What they are effectively saying, and sometimes even explicitly stating, is that God's Word is not enough; we need outside help. Scripture is insufficient to fully understand and deal with racism, partiality, justice, and reconciliation. An extra-biblical consultant is required to answer these real questions in the real world. I appreciate how Voddie Baucham describes this in his book *Fault Lines,*

> "The general theme of the current CSJ movement within evangelicalism is a covert attack on the sufficiency of Scripture. People are not coming right out and saying that the Bible is not enough. Instead, high-profile pastors get up and speak about the ways in which modern sociology texts have done for them what revelation of Scripture has been unable to do."[1]

Truth be known, those importing these ideas into Christianity are borrowing notions from a pagan worldview that hates Christianity. How sadly ironic. And if you've been wondering why so many Christians sound like the world it's because they are quoting worldly philosophies. As they do, they are leading themselves and others away from the only genuine source of truth and help.

What happens when those compromising with CRT are confronted with the reality of the anti-biblical worldview informing their borrowed ideas? Often the response is a casual don't worry we can just "eat the meat and spit out the bones." Or put another way, CRT is just a "helpful analytical tool." But if you eat poisonous meat you're still going to be poisoned, no

---

1   Voddie Baucham, *Fault Lines: The Social Justice Movement and Evangelicalism's Looming Catastrophe* (New York, NY: Salem Books, 2021), 125.

matter how many bones you spit out. And as defined early on, CRT is an all-encompassing toxic worldview, not some neutral tool like a telescope to be used sporadically.

Some will say the "social science" of critical race theory has just guided them to a different, better interpretation of biblical texts but hasn't replaced biblical authority. This is typically followed by a variation of an argument heard repeatedly here at Answers in Genesis. That Christians have diverse views of baptism, speaking in tongues, eschatology and so forth, so can't they have different views on justice and reconciliation?[2] The short answer is no, not consistently at least. You see, for issues like eschatology (the study of end times), what you typically have are various Christians comparing scripture with scripture. Of course, there are some extreme outlier views that are totally unbiblical. But for the most part it's Christians staying within the Word of God, comparing different Bible verses, and reaching various conclusions.[3] The major point is they're remaining anchored to the Bible. This is not how you get the CRT infused

---

2   Just replace "justice and reconciliation" with "Genesis" and you've got the common argument heard at AiG. And, as it turns out, the answer is the same for both. Here's an article as an example of how we normally deal with this relating to Genesis: "Are Different Views of Genesis the Same as Different Views of the End Times?", https://answersingenesis.org/blogs/ken-ham/2023/02/14/are-different-views-genesis-same-end-times/.

3   And, of course, there is only one right understanding of baptism, speaking in tongues, eschatology, etc. But that is not the point here nor is it within the scope of this book to focus on those issues.

views of justice and reconciliation being adopted by Christians today. The only way to reach those conclusions is to start with ideas outside of the Bible and use them to reinterpret the Bible. Consequently, man's word becomes the ultimate authority as the clear meaning of the biblical text is rejected in favor of a Neo-Marxist imported interpretation.

Of course, this is not to say the knowledge and understanding cannot be gained from various studies, research, and experience. It is to say, that everything is to be understood in relation to, and rest under the authority of, the Word of God. Again, either God's Word is supreme, or man's word is. Neutrality does not exist.

As established all throughout the book, these two incompatible world-views are at war with each other. Built on diametrically opposed foundations, they possess radically different views of man's identity, problem, and solution. CRT vehemently rejects the biblical narrative of man's identity and value, humanity's universal sin problem, and mankind's sole solution found at the cross. By doing so, CRT is a blatant attack on biblical authority, biblical anthropology, sufficiency of Scripture, and the sufficiency of the Gospel. CRT is an irredeemably broken ideology that is antithetical to the biblical worldview in about every way imaginable. Its tenets cannot be harmonized with the Bible, nor can they be justified with a veneer of "Christianese." The only right response to CRT dogmas is to

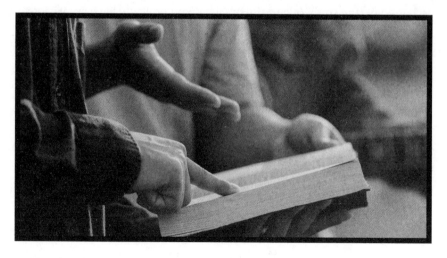

reject and refute them wherever they may be found. Dear Christian, we do not need the ideas of finite, sinful men, rooted in a pagan, anti-Christian worldview, to answer biblically defined and answered issues.

Christians can rest and rejoice in the glorious certainty that God's Word is forever sufficient.

> *Forever, O LORD, your word is firmly fixed in the heavens.*
> *(Psalm 119:89)*

Believers can also take comfort in the truth my beautiful bride pointed out as we discussed CRT together, that there is nothing new under the sun (Ecclesiastes 1:9). Today's societal issues of racism and reconciliation are not some brand-new things that God didn't see coming, for which an outside expert is required. Nor is the threat of CRT's destructive ideology unique in history. It's just another variation of the same old Genesis 3, "Did God really say?" attack. And the answer for today is the same as it has always been,

> *Trust in the LORD with all your heart,*
> *and do not lean on your own understanding.*
> *In all your ways acknowledge him, and he will make*
> *straight your paths (Proverbs 3:5–6).*

And how do we discern the ways of God and lean on His understanding? By going to His sure, perfect, and sufficient Word.

> *Through your precepts I get understanding; therefore I hate*
> *every false way. Your word is a lamp to my feet and light to*
> *my path. (Psalm 119:104–105)*

Some will undoubtedly respond, "But the Bible doesn't address all the specific details and nuances of our current societal situation." True, but it does something so much better and amazing. The Bible alone provides the only consistent foundation, framework, and standard to correctly address all of humanity's issues past, present, and future. For all human history, God's Word is sufficient regardless of the intricacies of any society or cultural issue. God's Word is eternally and universally true, applicable, and adequate. I mean, it's the Word of the living, eternal, majestic God. How could it be anything less (2 Peter 1:16–21)? And God assures us in His divine revelation,

> All Scripture is breathed out by God and profitable for teaching, for reproof, for correction, and for training in righteousness, that the man of God may be complete, equipped for every good work. (2 Timothy 3:16–17)

Through the applied Word of God rightly divided, believers in Christ can be fully armed and prepared to deal with every issue, including the issues of partiality and justice. When you break it down, justice by definition is a righteousness issue and Scripture literally trains Christians in righteousness. Thus, Christians are the prime candidates to address matters of justice. The "breathed out" Word of God equips followers of Christ for "every good work," including the good works of justice and reconciliation. Add to that the magnificent truths revealed in 2 Peter 1:3–4,

> His divine power has granted to us all things that pertain to life and godliness, through the knowledge of him who called us to his own glory and excellence, by which he has granted to us his precious and very great promises, so that through them you may become partakers of the divine nature, having escaped from the corruption that is in the world because of sinful desire.

God's "divine power" has given us everything we need pertaining to "life and godliness." Not some things or most things — everything. And by God's grace, Christians are miraculously partakers of "the divine nature" and have been set free from the bondage of sin. Of course we are not perfect this side of heaven, but we are no longer enslaved to sinful desires or sinful perceptions. We are indwelled by the Holy Spirit and have been given the mind of Christ (1 Corinthians 2:12–16). What else do we need!? Answer, nothing. God is enough. His Word is sufficient! There's literally no better source, no other right source, to use when addressing any issue, including the matters of racism, reconciliation, and justice.

Let us make sure that the world is not conforming us to its image or that we are being held hostage by a deceptive philosophy (Romans 12:2, Colossians 2:8). Instead, out of love for God and neighbor, may we *"destroy arguments and every lofty opinion raised against the knowledge of God."* Taking every thought captive to obey Christ and earnestly contending for the faith (2 Corinthians 10:5, Jude 1:3).

Dear Christian, there is nothing to fear. God's Word is sure, Jesus is on His throne, eternal victory is secure, and we possess the answers our culture is looking for. Let us boldly stand on God's Word and be the salt, light, and testimony of true reconciliation and justice our culture so desperately needs.[4]

---

4   For those who would like further practical instruction on how to apply God's sufficient Word to be anti-racist in the biblical (rather than CRT) sense, check out chapter 7 of the book *One Race One Blood* by Dr. Charles Ware entitled "Grace Relations": https://answersingenesis.org/racism/grace-relations/. The whole book, co-authored by Ken Ham and Dr. Charles Ware, is fantastic and worth reading. Also, Dr. Ware's *Grace Relations* series on Answers.TV is another wonderful resource.

Appendix: God's Word vs. Marx's word

As a helpful tool and resource, here is a quick reference chart comparing the biblical worldview to the Marxist/Neo-Marxist pagan ideology that drives CRT (and the modern LGBTQ+ revolution). Of course, it is not exhaustive but concisely covers key points. This chart was published in an article on the Answers in Genesis website and is used with full permission. It was co-authored by myself and Patricia Engler, fellow Answers in Genesis speaker and author of the fantastic book *Modern Marxism* which I highly recommend.[1]

Seven Major Conflicts Between God's Word and Marxism

Worldview Topic	Biblical View	Marxist View (or Neo-Marxist)
Human origins	God supernaturally created humans in His image. (Genesis 1:26-27)	Humans arose through natural processes.
Human nature	Humans are created (Genesis 2:7, 21-23; Psalm 100:3)	Humans are primarily *creators.*
Identity	Identity primarily defined by and rooted in Christ. (Galatians 3:28)	Identity primarily defined by and rooted in certain traits (gender, income, skin-tone, etc.).

1   https://answersingenesis.org/culture/marxism-false-gospel-appealing-liberal-churches/

Worldview Topic	Biblical View	Marxist View (or Neo-Marxist)
Human marriage and family	God ordained marriage between a husband and wife as part of His very good design for creation, and as the basis for raising and discipling children. The family is the foundational unit of society. (Deuteronomy 6:7, Matthew 19:4-5)	Marriage and family are pillars of an oppressive social system and need to be redefined, manipulated, or abolished.
Humanity's core problem	The problem comes down to sin. (Genesis 2:17 and 3:1-24, Romans 5:12)	The problem comes down to economic or cultural conditions.
Guilt	Guilt is based on sin against God. All people are guilty by nature before God, apart from Christ. (Psalm 53:3, Ecclesiastes 7:20, Romans 3:23, 1 John 1:10)	Guilt is based on identity. People with "oppressor" identities are automatically guilty and cannot help being evil; people with "oppressed" identities are automatically innocent and can do no evil.
Humanity's hope of redemption	Salvation is found only in Jesus. (Acts 4:12, Romans 10:9)	Salvation is found only through revolution.

Additional Differences:

Topic	Biblical View	Marxist View (or Neo-Marxist)
Truth	Truth is objective. God is the source of authority for truth. (John 14:6, John 17:17)	Truth is subjective. The feelings and lived experience of the oppressed are the authority for truth.
Morality	The standard and foundation for morality is God's character. Morals can be known through God's Word and God's law written on our consciousness. (Psalm 119:68, Romans 2:15)	The standard for morality is whatever tilts the power balance in favor of the oppressed.
Oppression	Oppression is a matter of committing wrongful actions against other image-bearers—especially vulnerable groups, including widows, orphans, and the poor. (Jeremiah 22:3–5, Isaiah 1:17 & 10:1–3, Zechariah 7:10, Malachi 3:5)	Oppression is a matter of belonging to an identity group with more or less power and privilege. People with "privileged" traits are oppressive by definition.

Topic	Biblical View	Marxist View (or Neo-Marxist)
Justice	Justice is primarily a matter of actions, attitudes, and personal character that accord with God's Word and nature. God is a just God who performs just actions. Biblical justice insists upon impartiality, righteousness in legal judgments, honest dealings, and the defense of the needy. (Leviticus 19:15, Psalm 82:3, Proverbs 11:1 and 31:9, Isaiah 1:17; Amos 5:15).	Justice is primarily a matter of disempowering the oppressors and empowering the oppressed.
Liberation	Freedom means being liberated from sin and its effects. (John 8:34-36, Romans 8:2)	Freedom means being liberated from social conditions that are oppressive (by the Marxist definition of oppressive).
Knowledge	God reveals truth through His Word and gave humans faculties for finding out, knowing, and reasoning about facts. (Psalm 119:66, Proverbs 2:6 and 18:15, James 1:5.)	The oppressed, as the authority for truth, are the authority for knowledge. The oppressed reveal knowledge which oppressors cannot otherwise learn.

Appendix: God's Word vs. Marx's word

Topic	Biblical View	Marxist View (or Neo-Marxist)
Human effort	Good works (as defined by God) are an indispensable reflection of lives transformed by Jesus. However, our good works don't save us and cannot ultimately redeem the world from its fallenness. (James 2:14-17, Ephesians 2:8-10)	Good works are defined as actions which help empower the oppressed or disempower oppressors. By bringing about the revolution, such works will ultimately redeem humanity from its problems.
Racism	There is only one human race (Acts 17:26). All forms of prejudice are evil (James 2:1), including ethnic prejudice (racism). Individuals are accountable for their own evil actions or attitudes (Ezekiel 18:1-20, 2 Kings 14:6, Matthew 16:27). The ultimate cause for prejudice is sin; the ultimate solution is the gospel.	According to CRT, people are either oppressors or oppressed based on "race." Only prejudice against oppressed "races" is evil. Individuals are automatically guilty or innocent based on their "racial" identity. "Racism" is systemic, pervading all social systems. Oppressor "races" benefit from these systems, so cannot help being racist, and members of an "oppressed" race cannot be racist by definition. The only solution is revolution.

Topic	Biblical View	Marxist View (or Neo-Marxist)
Gender and Sexuality	God made humans male and female (Genesis 1:26, Mark 10:6-9). These two genders are distinct, complementary, and equally image God. Biological sex and gender are equivalent and inseparable. Gender and sexuality are good gifts from our Creator for human flourishing, when applied according to His design.	As self-creators, humans define their own gender. Biological sex does not necessarily determine gender or sexual orientation. Gender binaries are artificial and oppressive. According to Critical Gender Theory, "cis-gender heterosexual maleness" is oppressive and must be overthrown.

Photo Credits: